THE HOME APPLIANCE CLINIC:

Controls, Cycle Timers, Wiring & Repair

No. 745
$7.95

THE HOME APPLIANCE CLINIC:

Controls, Cycle Timers, Wiring & Repair

by Jack Darr

TAB BOOKS
Blue Ridge Summit, Pa. 17214

PREFACE

There may be a great deal more to consider when checking out a major appliance than the circuit of the appliance itself. A major electrical appliance draws a great deal of current; and a high current drain generally means more attention must be paid to wiring sizes, lengths of wire runs, voltage drops, and the like. A gas appliance has fewer parts to malfunction, of course, but when one of the parts does go bad, it has to be repaired.

This book is intended to bridge the gap between an elementary repair job and installation of electrical or gas service. Its focus is on control systems (valving in the case of gas appliances, and switching / timing sequences in the case of the larger electrical appliances). In covering the gamut, the author has included information on some traditionally hard-to-service items, such as floor polisher-scrubbers, electrostatic air cleaners, electronic cigarette lighters, ground fault interrupters, and other circuits that can't readily be categorized as either major or small appliances.

The material presented here appeared first in the pages of **Radio-Electronics** magazine as the Home Appliance Clinic. It is unprecedented success may be attributable in part to the author's inimitable style, but the overall range of coverage and depth of information combine to make the material virtually timeless and almost universally applicable.

This isn't the sort of book that requires straight-through reading. Each chapter is complete in itself. When you run into difficulty on a repair job, just look up the appropriate entries in the index, then go right to the referenced chapter.

If you're comparatively new to appliance servicing, it might pay you to read the appendix material (page 179), which offers all the information you'll ever need to understand and use effectively the indispensible multimeter. This appendix is a reprint from a U.S. Government publication written for military electrical and electronic troubleshooters.

The Editors

CONTENTS

Home Appliance Electronics ① 1

Say "electronics" and we usually think of TV, radio, and the like. However, you'll find electronic circuits, principles, and gadgetry being used more and more in things other than the entertainment uses we are familiar with. You'd be surprised at how many purely electronic (as compared to strictly "electric") things and applications you can find now.

If you'll check, you'll find that the electronic circuits used are extremely simple. At least, they look simple to the guy who spends his days digging around in the bewildering complexity of color TV, stereo decoders, ultrasonic remote control systems, and their ilk.

Maytag Co., of Newton, Iowa, probably the oldest maker of washers and dryers in the country, has been using a very simple, purely electronic control circuit on automatic dryers for some time. The basic circuit is in the diagram of Fig. 1-1. It provides an automatic cutoff for the dryer for different types of fabrics.

The circuit action is as follows; when the unit goes into the timed phase of the **dry** cycle, the rectifier is switched into the circuit. This develops a dc voltage which is applied to the capacitor through one of several different-value resistors. The correct resistor is selected by one of the pushbutton switches on the panel.

The capacitor starts to charge. The time constant of this, of course, is plain old "RC"—the value of the resistor multiplied by that of the capacitor. The result is the time (in seconds) for the dry cycle.

A neon lamp is connected to the capacitor. As most of us know, these lamps fire at about 67 volts. The other side of the

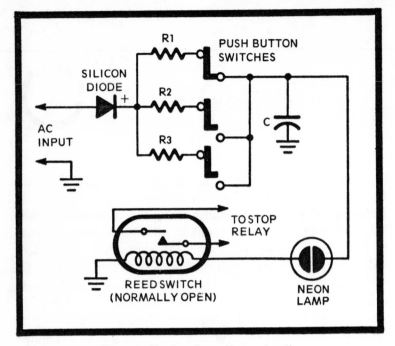

Fig. 1-1. Maytag dryer timer circuit.

lamp returns to ground through the coil of a reed switch. It takes only a very small current pulse to make these switches close.

When the dc voltage on the capacitor has reached the necessary level, the neon lamp fires. This allows a small pulse of current to flow through the reed-switch coil, closing the contacts. When these contacts close, they actuate another (heavier) relay, which has been holding the heating elements, motor, etc. on while the dryer runs. This relay now opens, stopping the dryer.

That's all there is to it. To get a longer running time, a larger resistor is switched in, and vice versa. This is about as simple as you can get, and it's worked for some years.

Most of the "home" electronics are equally basic. You'll find quite a number of different things, from triac lamp dimmers to timing controls of different kinds, temperature controls, and on and on.

Varispeed Thyristor Control Devices

A friend and I were looking at the diagrams of some new appliances. My friend looked at something labeled SCR and said, "SCR? Speed Control Resistor?"

I said, "No, but you're about as close as you could get and still be wrong. That's what it does all right; but it's real name is **silicon controlled rectifier**.

"That sounds a little silly," said my friend. "You mean the rectifier is controlled by silicon?" An SCR is a diode rectifier that may be controlled with a low-current voltage applied to its gate terminal. It's made from silicon, like most diodes capable of handling fairly heavy loads and withstanding reasonably high temperatures. Thus its name. Probably the device would have some other handle if it were being named today...like **gated power diode** or **dc pulsed switch**. But SCR has stuck—and we're stuck with it.

Since we're going to see quite a lot of these things in modern appliances, used for speed control and switching, it'd be a good idea to try and work up a plain-language explanation of how they work.

Let's begin with a plain old silicon diode—yep, a rectifier. If we feed an ac voltage into it, we get half-wave rectification; one half-cycle of the ac voltage is clipped off, as in Fig. 2-1. Since the power in an ac waveform includes both positive and negative half-cycles, the output would have only half the input power.

If we wanted less than that, we could use a special type of diode—the SCR. The basic SCR is a single diode and works just like any other; but—this one has a built-in switch. It is called a

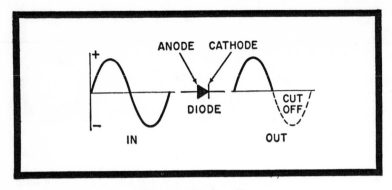

Fig. 2-1. Diode action.

gate, and for good reason. When the gate is closed, the SCR will not conduct at all—in either direction. Figure 2-2 shows what would happen if we "opened the gate"—connected a voltage to it so the SCR conducts at all times.

So, a turned-on SCR works just like all diodes. Full-wave in, half-wave out. (Yes, I know it's dc!) If we want to use the gate as a power-output control, we add a trigger circuit, so that the gate turns the SCR on at a given point during the positive half-cycle. Figure 2-3 shows what we'd have if this was at the positive peak. There would be no current flow at all until the point where the SCR turns on; and from there on the cycle would be of normal shape. In a circuit like this, we'd get about ¼ of the total input power, since we've already clipped off a whole half-cycle.

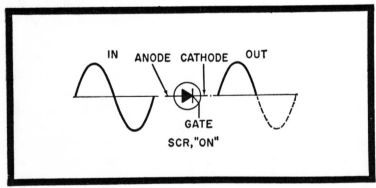

Fig. 2-2. SCR with gate voltage applied.

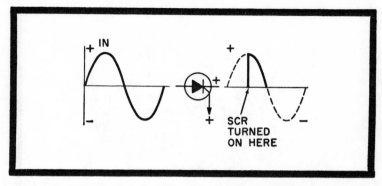

Fig. 2-3. An SCR can be turned on at any point during an input cycle.

This is fine (and is actually used in certain circuits such as battery chargers), but it's not too handy for such uses as speed control of electrical appliances with motors. So, we use a special device which is actually two SCRs connected in reverse parallel to form a **triac**. Figure 2-4 shows the symbol for this. You can see the two diodes, one looking each way. This triac also has a gate, which controls both diodes. Each one can be gated on when the applied polarity of the voltage is correct. In Fig. 2-4, the upper half of the triac would conduct during the positive half-cycle, and the lower half during the negative half-cycle. (All diodes conduct when the anode is positive with respect to the cathode.) Figure 2-4 shows what we'd have if the triac were gated on at all times: the output is the same as the input.

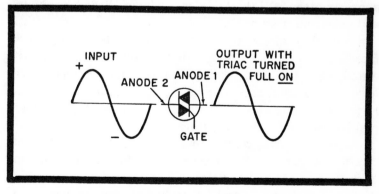

Fig. 2-4. The triac is really reverse paralleled SCRs.

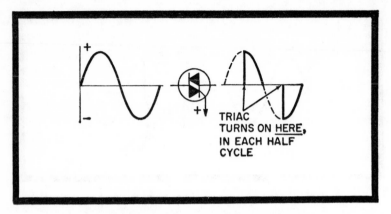

Fig. 2-5. Triac-controlled ac waveform.

To make this practical, we simply add a trigger circuit, which will vary the point where the triac is gated on. So if we set the control to get half-speed, our output waveform would look something like Fig. 2-5. We're getting half of each input half-cycle in the output, and thus half the current. Halving the current and voltage results in a quartering of the power, since power is a fraction of the product of voltage and current ($P = EI$).

Figure 2-6 shows a complete control circuit of the basic type you'll find in a lot of appliances. The variable 100,000-ohm resistor applies the voltage to the resistor-capacitor network. During each half-cycle, the voltage on the .05 uF capacitor builds up as the input voltage rises. When it reaches a value of approximately 28V, the "bilateral trigger diode" conducts and gates the triac on.

The bilateral trigger diode is referred to by engineers these days as a **diac**. In construction, the device is almost exactly like a triac with the gate element removed. Insensitive to voltage polarity, the diac conducts by going into a negative-resistance region at a specified input voltage that is either positive, negative, or alternating.

The name **triac** comes from an acronym of **trigger** and alternating current. For a short time after the device's introduction, it was called "**trigac**." The name **diac** comes from diode and ac. The only real similarity between the diac and a diode, though, is the fact that the diac does indeed have but two terminals.

The circuit of Fig. 2-6 is that of a conventional lamp dimmer, but it is also found as a speed control for certain types of appliance motors, too.

The charging time of a capacitor in such a circuit depends on the amount of series resistance in the charging circuit. So the setting of the 100,000-ohm pot determines the time needed for the capacitor to reach the diac's firing voltage.

In a different version of this circuit, a small neon lamp is used in place of the trigger diode. These lamps will "fire" (glow) whenever the applied voltage reaches approximately 68 volts. A diac may fire at substantially less voltage, so it is more common than the neon. The circuit of Fig. 2-6 uses a diac that fires at 32V. A neon lamp is an open circuit until it fires. This allows a pulse of voltage to pass and reach the triac gate. The lamp will fire once during each half-cycle, so once again we get full-wave control action.

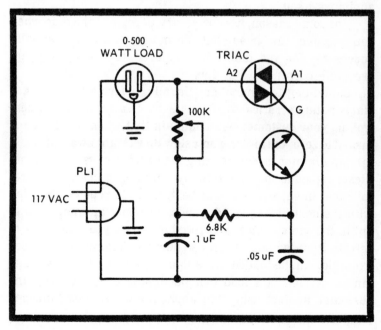

Fig. 2-6. Triac-diac lamp dimmer.

You'll find these things used in multiple-speed blenders; variable-speed electric drills; multispeed electric mixers, and so on. In a lot of cases, they'll be sealed up in "black boxes," but if you have some idea what they're supposed to do, you can check them. They won't be too easy to check with an ohmmeter, for example, but you can almost always "jumper" a speed-control device. If the motor runs or the device operates, but it won't with the speed control device in circuit, that's it; replace it.

Excessive loads cause the triac to fail, but the other components in the circuit are usually still fully functional. If you can get into the black box, you can ordinarily replace the triac with little difficulty. The most important criterion when ordering a replacement triac is its current-handling capacity, but of course maximum voltage must also be considered. The conventional replacement triac is a 600-watt device, but the maximum rating cannot be achieved without having the triac mounted in a heatsink of some sort—usually the case of the appliance itself.

For some reason, it's customary to replace the diac when you replace the triac—but normally this isn't actually necessary, for the diac isn't required to convey any appreciable current in a circuit.

Something to remember: Usually, before a triac fails, it starts acting erratically. If the device is a motor speed controller, your customer will complain that when the device is turned to zero, the motor won't slow down right away. If it's in a lamp dimmer circuit, setting it to zero results in the lamp flickering some, but not actually dimming much for several minutes. In such cases, your best bet is to replace the triac with the next higher rated device. The only alternative is to put in the same device as before but advise your customer to refrain from loading the unit so heavily. A lamp dimmer, for example, can be loaded more lightly by using lower-wattage lamps. A blender's load can be lightened by advising the customer against using the appliance on viscous "mashed potato" loads.

Time-Constant Circuits

Electrical appliances, industrial electronics apparatus, and a lot of common things make use of electronic principles. Most of these are old hat to us but may be pretty strange to other people. The applications of ordinary, simple electronic principles are many and varied. None of them will be complicated, if you know your electronic ABCs. Look for these, and you'll find a lot of things that you can fix! Some of the uses for these might surprise you.

A good example of this is a job that I got rung in on not too long ago. A friend was working on an automatic door opener—you know the thing, where you step on the little mat in front and the door opens without you even having to say "Open, Sesame"? This one was working, but the door opened as soon as you stepped on the mat, and then it chased you through! If you were fast enough, you could make it ahead of the door, which started to close instantly!

Since this was the door that let the customers into the store, the manager was understandably upset. So, we began checking. I said (prophetically, it turned out), "Sure has a short time-constant." It did. According to the instruction book, the door was supposed to open, hold for a minimum of three seconds, then close. (This being a new piece of gear to both of us, we did it the hard way—we read the instruction book first!)

The door itself was operated by a hydraulic mechanism, which was obviously working fine. The control was a nice simple two-tube electronic circuit, using 6V6s. Figure 3-1 shows the schematic. The sequence was started when you stepped on the mat; this closed a switch, and this in turn closed relay RY1.

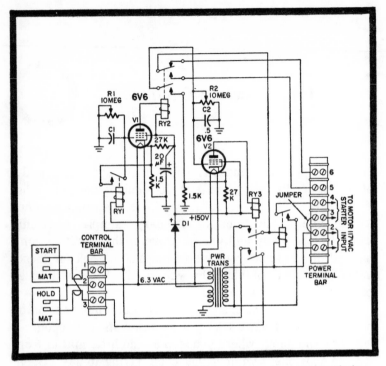

Fig. 3-1. Electronically triggered door opener for supermarkets.

When the contacts of RY1 close, a positive voltage, coming from V1 cathode and a dropping resistor to the dc power supply, is applied to the grid. Plate current flows, and relay RY2 closes, doing the same thing for tube V2, which in turn closes RY3 in its plate circuit. This controls the solenoid valve which actually switches the door mechanism. It also starts a pump to supply the hydraulic pressure. All of this was obviously working very well, since the door did open and close. The problem was in the timing.

This is controlled by the grid voltage of V1. When the positive voltage is applied, it charges capacitor C1, 0.5 uF from grid to ground. When you step off the mat, opening the circuit, RY1 opens. The charge on C1 now leaks off through variable resistor R1. The time needed for the grid voltage to drop to the point where the tube stops drawing current is determined by the setting of R1.

This is the "time constant" of this circuit. To find out exactly how much delay you'd get, simply multiply the capacitance of C1 in microfarads by the resistance of R1 in megohms, and you come out with the time, in seconds. Here, the resistor was 10 megohms and the capacitor 0.5 uF, so the maximum time constant should be 5 seconds. This, we didn't have, so I took the "electronics" out, and went to the bench with it.

After connecting it, I turned it on and jumpered mat-switch contacts 1 and 2. The relays closed, and the grid voltage of each tube jumped to about +15 volts (read with a 15-megohm-input multimeter). Tube V2 held as it should; however, the grid voltage of V1 dropped off very rapidly! When it got down to about +3 volts, RY1 opened. Several seconds later, RY2 opened, after the V2 grid had fallen to the same value.

I smiled (very pleased and mildly astonished) and disconnected the charging capacitor on the grid of V1. Sure enough, this showed a fairly high leakage on the insulation resistance test of my capacitor tester. An ohmmeter wouldn't show this, since the total leakage was in the order of several megohms.

I replaced it, after carefully checking the new one for leakage. Now this tube would hold its grid voltage up for several seconds, and the variable resistor would adjust the time constant between about 7 and 2 seconds. This was just what we wanted. So I replaced the other one, too, just for luck.

When you run into something that you've never seen before, look it over carefully. The chances are that you'll find some "old friends" in the way of simple electronic circuits just like this. If so, by applying your basic knowledge of electronics, you'll be able to figure out just how they work.

You may have to go back to your basic electronics texts to remember what a time constant is all about. Sometimes I think we get so used to thinking of building charges that we forget that a time constant is just as applicable to charge leakoff. A time constant is the time it takes for a capacitor to charge to a value equal to 63.2 percent of its maximum. It takes five such time constants for a capacitor to charge to 99 percent of full value. But it also takes five full time constants for a capacitor's charge to leak away in an RC circuit. The first such time constant leaks away all but 36.8 percent of the capacitor's charge. By the end of the second time constant, the capacitor's charge is only 13.5 percent of maximum; at 3t it's at 5 percent; at 4t it's at 2 percent; and at 5t, the capacitor's charge is but 1 percent of the full-charge maximum.

There's another familiar circuit in Fig. 3-1; look at the dc power supply! Silicon diode half-wave rectifier (D1) with a 20 uF electrolytic filter capacitor. If the filter capacitor should open, the unit wouldn't work, because of low plate voltage. The diode could also open or short; in other words, same old type of trouble you'd find in any ac-dc radio!

You'll find this kind of application, of simple electronic circuitry, used in quite a few things. You can fix them with ease if you'll look them over carefully, and make sure that all of the "necessaries" are present; dc voltage, good parts, tubes, transistors, etc. You won't find any new things; just the same old things used for different purposes.

Electrostatic Air Cleaner

Clean air has become a very popular slogan lately. And in many localities, there's no doubt that there is a need for it. Our air is often loaded with particulate matter of all shapes, sizes, and degrees of toxicity! This contamination must be removed before the air is circulated through the building, whether this is a home or a huge office building.

In the past this has been done by plain old sticky-filters— shallow boxes filled with porous materials, coated with some kind of oil, etc., that catch the dust particles. The efficiency of such a system is fair. However, there is a better way, with electronics.

If a high-intensity electrical charge is put on a particle, by passing it through an electric field, it will then be attracted to any object with an opposite-polarity charge. So if we put a high positive charge on the dust particles by forcing them through a metal grid with a high-voltage charge, they will then be highly attracted to a negatively charged grid.

They will be precipitated out of the air. Air cleaners that work on this principle are known as precipitators. In use, the air passes through the two grids made of thin metal rods, etc. These are mounted very close to either side of a standard filter. Particles are charged as they pass through the first grid and precipitated onto the second.

This makes cleaning simple. Nothing holds the particles to the second grid, except the charge. If it is discharged, the grid can be shaken or tapped lightly and the dust falls off. The grid is then ready for use again. In some of the more elaborate units, periodic discharging and jarring are done automatically so the unit remains at high efficiency at all times.

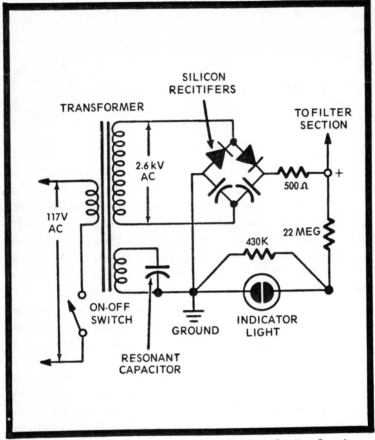

Fig. 4-1. Electrostatic air cleaner. (Courtesy Carrier Corp.)

Circuitry

Once again, here's a plain, standard electronic circuit. A power transformer supplies 2.6 kV ac to a full-wave (symmetrical) voltage-doubler rectifier circuit (see Fig. 4-1). The doubler capacitors are connected as usual, with the other end of the power transformer secondary to their midpoint. A 500-ohm surge resistor is connected between the high-voltage output (5.2 kV) and the lines to the filter grids. This protects the rectifiers against accidental shorts between grids.

A 22-megohm load resistor is connected from the high-voltage terminal to ground (negative side of the circuit).

There is a 430,000-ohm resistor between the ground end of the big resistor and the actual ground. The 100-volt drop across this resistor lights a neon lamp. There is no normal current in this circuit, of course. It uses the high electrostatic fields. Current is limited to 5 mA by a special resonant protection circuit on the power transformer.

It consists of a tertiary winding with a capacitor across it. If the current goes over 5 mA, the capacitor and tertiary winding act to oversaturate the core, thus holding the current down.

If the filters become clogged with dust or dirt so that there is a leakage between the positive and negative grids, the high voltage will drop, and the indicator neon lamp will go out, showing that the unit is no longer working. When the precipitator is turned off, the resistors discharge the high voltage so the grids can be taken out for cleaning without a shock hazard to the technician. Even while it is working, the 5.2 kV voltage can give you an annoying bite, but there is little current and no danger of lethal shocks.

Replacement Parts

All electronic parts used are now standard, outside of the power transformer. The rectifiers could be replaced by stock color-TV focus rectifiers, since the applied voltage is well within their ratings. High-voltage capacitors are available in all sizes now. The doublers are tubular types. The resonating capacitor is a bathtub type.

In this unit, the power transformer is a specially encased type, probably an epoxy case. The case has wells for the doubler capacitors and grooves for the rectifiers, resistors, etc., and push-on terminals for connecting the primary, high-voltage, and indicator lamp leads. The resonating capacitor is mounted on one side of this case.

The grid-filter unit will vary in size and shape, but functionally they're all the same. Figure 4-2 shows a schematic layout of this kind of unit. (Spacing between the grids and filter have been exaggerated to show construction.)

This is still another instance of how we can make use of the very basic principles of electronics to do things. Any elec-

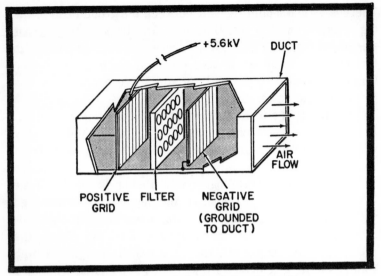

Fig. 4-2. Construction of electrostatic air purifier.

tronics technician can repair such things with ease if he remembers his basic theory and uses a little ingenuity in selecting replacement parts. These are often available, off-the-shelf, in parts houses!

IONIZER

Researchers working with air-conditioning discovered that the ion content of the air was important. This was especially true in cases of hay fever and other respiratory ailments, certain allergies, and so on. Indoor air in particular was found to have a shortage of negative ions. Normal outdoor air was well balanced in that respect. Restoring the ion balance of indoor air gave relief to the sufferers.

Philco developed a device which would feed negative ions into the air of a room. Beside this, the air was forced through a filter and treated with a germicidal agent. This removed dust, pollen, etc., which also helped. The basic principle of this is very familiar to electronics technicians; we see it all the time!

The complete circuit is in Fig. 4-3. You'll recognize it right away! About 1000 volts ac is provided by a small power transformer. This is fed to a standard voltage-tripler, which

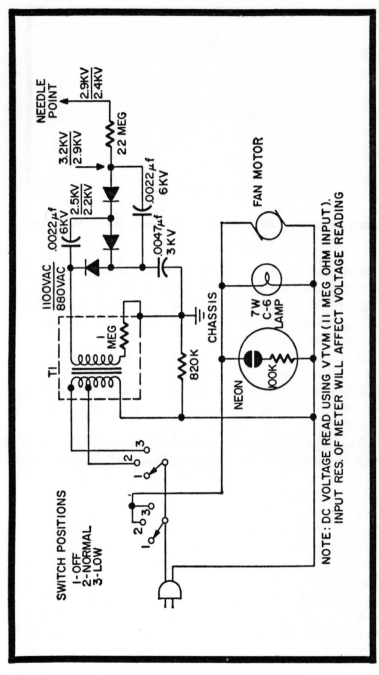

Fig. 4-3. Philco electronic air ionizer.

27

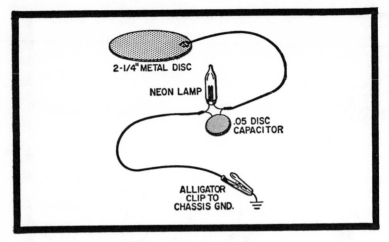

2-1/4" METAL DISC

NEON LAMP

.05 DISC CAPACITOR

ALLIGATOR CLIP TO CHASSIS GND.

Fig. 4-4. Philco's tester.

develops about 3 kV. This voltage, negative in polarity, is connected to a long, thin metal needle, mounted in a plastic insulator. The insulator is positioned in the center of a plastic duct, called the stack, with the air forced up through this by the fan (after being filtered).

As the air passes the sharp point of the needle, negative ions are discharged into it and the air-stream carries them throughout the room. This is very familiar to us. We've often seen corona discharges from highly charged sharp points in HV circuits!

The only moving part in this unit is a small electric motor driving a fan or squirrel-cage blower. It is about the same size as the motors used in phonographs and could probably be replaced by one of these, if necessary.

The electronics are very simple. Three solid-state rectifiers are used. These are the same type as the solid-state focus rectifiers used in color TV sets. The filter capacitors are small, 2 to 3 kV rated ceramic disc types. A 22-megohm resistor is connected between the tripler output and the discharge needle. Since this is strictly a voltage device, there is negligible current flowing. The high-value resistor prevents the chance of serious shock if the needle tip is accidentally touched.

Checking these units can be very easy. Any HV probe used with a very high impedance TVM or VTVM will read the 3 kV voltage on the needle.

Philco also shows a homemade tester for this unit (Fig. 4-4).

The lamp is an NE-2; the capacitor, anything from 0.05 to 0.1 uF. The bigger the capacitor, the slower the rate of flashing. A 2-inch metal plate is connected to one side of the lamp-capacitor circuit, and a ground lead, with clip, to the other. Fasten the clip to the chassis, and hold the metal plate over (but not touching) the tip of the needle. If the neon lamp flashes continuously, the thing is working.

If you find there is no HV, the rectifiers can be checked by substitution. The dc HV can be traced through the tripler circuit to find out where it stops multiplying. Most troubles will be bad rectifiers or shorted or leaky capacitors. Incidentally, the voltage-multiplier circuit will be found in quite a few late-model color TV sets! If rectifiers are bad, it should be possible to replace them with a stock color-TV tripler.

All parts should be easy to replace with stock TV parts. The exception would be the power transformer. It might be replaced by a small oscilloscope power transformer. Check transformer catalogs.

5

Failsafe Devices

Every automatic appliance, and especially the types which heat things, is (or darn well should be!) equipped with failsafe controls. By definition, this means that if anything fails that could cause a dangerous condition to exist, the thing shuts itself off and won't operate at all. This covers such dangerous things as escaping gas, electrical arcing, and any other hazardous condition.

This is especially important on any gas-fired heating appliance; heaters, furnaces, boilers, clothes dryers, and so on. All of these are now made with automatic controls. The controls operate electrically. The main gas valve is always a solenoid type. So, all of the safeties are keyed to this control. Unless they all indicate Safe!, the main gas valve will not open; so no unburnt gas can escape into the house.

Failsafe units are mostly electrically operated, although there are pressure operated, temperature operated, and other types. They all do one thing: open or close a switch! This switch closes if the unit senses normal operating conditions; if not, it shuts everything down until the trouble is found and cleared up. All of the safety switches are connected in series, between the power supply and the main gas valve.

A typical example of a really complex system is shown in Fig. 5-1. This is the actual circuit of a good-sized gas-fired boiler for a steam heating system. Everything which could cause trouble is protected by a failsafe sensor. Here you can see how several different types of sensors are used. The **high gas** and **low gas** sensors check the input pressure, usually between limits of 4 and 8 oz.

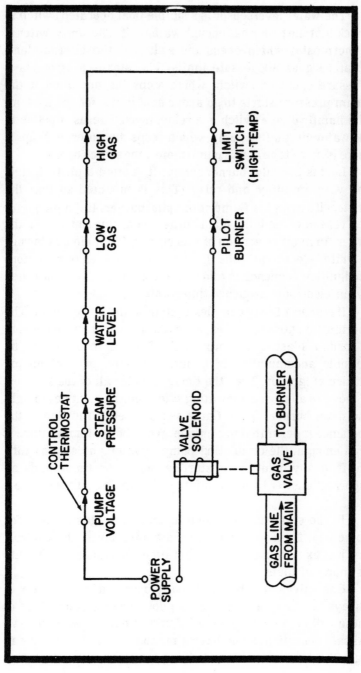

Fig. 5-1. Gas line failsafe switching.

The **water level** sensor is a simple float operated switch to check that the boiler has enough water in it. The **limit switch** is a thermostat which opens the switch if the internal temperature goes above safe limits. The **steam pressure** is a pressure operated switch, which stops the operation if the steam pressure starts to go above safe limits for the system. The **pump voltage** switch is a relay, hooked across the line to the water circulation pump, which keeps the water level up. If there is no voltage at this pump motor, the switch opens.

Last is the **pilot burner** safety. It is often a photoelectric cell with amplifier and relay. This is mounted so that the photocell senses the flame of the **pilot** burner. If it goes out for any reason (even if the main burner is on) this shuts down the boiler. In another version of this circuit, the main gas burner is ignited electrically; the flame sensor must see flame before the ignition sequence is allowed to continue. (It is controlled by an electronic sequence-timer unit.)

It can be a fairly complex system in the larger units. The thermostat starts the timer, which first starts a purge blower; it sends a blast of air through the firebox, to blow out any possible accumulation of unburnt gas and prevent an explosion at ignition. Then the timer samples all of the safeties. If they are all closed, indicating safe conditions, it tries to light the main burner. If the flame sensor "sees" the flame, the sequence is permitted to continue. When boiler temperature is high enough, the circulating pumps (water and steam) turn on. If at any point in the start sequence the timer finds an incorrect answer from the safeties, the whole thing comes to a halt.

In the smaller units, such as automatic gas heaters for home use, furnaces, and air-conditioning units, the controls are just exactly the same in operation. But there aren't quite as many of them!

Gas valves are still electrically operated, and there will always be one type of safety: a pilot-burner sensor. None of these will come on if the pilot flame is out. So we still have failsafe operation. Some have a manual override, so you can light the burner by hand, holding the gas valve open. This should be used merely to be sure that there is adequate gas pressure, etc, but only for testing. The failsafe devices should never be jumpered out.

There are two major types of these safeties on the pilot burner. Both use a special thermocouple, which is mounted on the main burner, but placed so that it is only in the pilot flame. It provides a very small dc voltage when heated to the proper temperature.

Two types of systems are used with these. In the oldest type, called a BASO pilot, the safety is a special relay mounted on the outside of the heater or furnace. The thermostat will not close this relay by itself; not enough voltage. However, when the manual knob on the relay is pushed down and held while the pilot burner is lit, it will stay closed. So this could be called a "manual set / automatic trip" system.

Power for operating the main gas valve, etc. is usually 24 volts ac, from a small transformer. The complete circuit is from the transformer through room-thermostat contacts, contacts on BASO pilot relay, through a high-temperature limit switch, then through the gas-valve solenoid and back to the transformer.

Now we come to another version—much smaller, but basically the same. All functions of the devices are exactly the same. There are not as many of them, and they're smaller, but they still control the system automatically and provide failsafe protection for the user. They are found on gas furnaces, gas dryers, space heaters, and that kind of thing.

The major difference lies in the fact that many of these are self-powered. There is no external 24-volt ac supply to operate the main gas valve. You will find "combination" systems, using thermocouple safeties plus the 24V ac valves in some units. However, the one we want to talk about here is the self-powered type. All of the electrical power needed to open the main gas valve is generated by a small thermocouple. The drawing of Fig. 5-2 shows the basic circuit.

The thermocouple itself is mounted on the side of the main burner, usually as a part of the pilot burner assembly. It must be here so it can sense the presence of the pilot flame. No flame, no voltage—which is the idea of the whole bit!

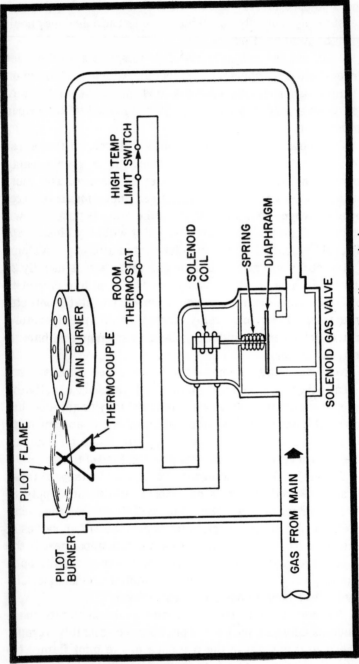

Fig. 5-2. Self-powered gas line control.

If you can see the pilot burner, you'll see that the thermocouple is positioned so it is right in the middle of the pilot flame. Some of the instructions refer to this as being in a ring of flame. This is necessary for maximum heating of the thermocouple.

The dc voltage generated is almost directly proportional to the heat. The pilot burner must be correctly adjusted for a nonblowing blue flame. That is, the pilot gas pressure should be adjusted so the flame does not blow away from the orifice. This lowers the temperature. If the pilot flame shows a distinct yellow tinge, it has too much air and not enough gas, and once again the temperature goes down. Instructions for adjusting this flame are in the service manuals. There will be an adjustment for the pilot flame on the side of the control unit itself.

The original application of this system used a manually set relay between the thermocouple and the gas-valve power supply. With the pilot burner lit, the relay is closed by pushing a button. If the thermocouple is working properly, it will hold the relay closed, although it will not close it. If the pilot burner should go out, the relay drops out, opening the circuit to the main gas valve. This is a manual-on / automatic-off system.

Millivolt Systems

Newer systems, especially on the small home-type heaters, operate on nothing but the minute voltage developed by the thermocouple. For obvious reasons, these are called millivolt systems, for that's what you'll read: millivolts! Gas valves are built with specially designed coils, so that they will open on very small currents. One that we checked, an ITT B60, needed only 30 mA dc from the thermocouple!

The valves themselves are specially designed with a very light diaphragm—usually of a special construction called a bleeder diaphragm. With it, the gas pressure itself actually helps to open and close the valve. The diaphragm is operated by the plunger (core) of the solenoid, and a light spring helps to push the diaphragm closed when the excitation is removed. Like all gas valves, they are normally closed. If power is taken away, they close, to shut off the gas (failsafe). Since the home gas lines work at a pressure of only a few ounces (4-6 oz is typical), this kind of operation is practical.

The drawing again shows the stock series circuit arrangement. The room thermostat closes when the temperature falls below the set level. The high-temperature limit switch is normally closed. If the plenum temperature rises above a certain level, it opens, shutting the system down.

Any of these units can be checked for proper electrical operation with a standard 20,000-ohm-per-volt meter. If the controls won't start the burner and gas pressure is okay, check the pilot flame. Also, see that the thermocouple body is right in the middle of the flame. If so, and the main burner refuses to light, start checking the electrical circuit.

Take a voltage reading across the output terminals of the thermocouple on the top of the control unit. Look for a minimum reading of about 70-80 mV. Most home-type thermocouples will have an output from this level up to perhaps 150-175 mV. There are high-power thermocouples which have outputs up to 800 mV or more, but most home-type units will probably be in the 150 mV region.

If you get no output at this point, disconnect the leads from the control unit and take a reading right across them. The meter can be left on the 1V range or switched to the 30 mA range. Here you should get an output of up to 30 mA if the thermocouple is in good shape.

No reading at all probably indicates a defective thermocouple. Try a new one. (Be sure that the original did have enough heat—that it is right in the middle of the pilot flame!) Incidentally, although this is dc, these units are not polarized. Leads can be connected either way. If some devices do need polarization, it will be indicated by color-coded leads.

If you do get what looks like a normal output from the thermocouple (still hooked up) but the gas valve won't open, take a voltage reading across the leads to the room thermostat. With such minute currents and voltages, we can't take any perceptible resistance in either switch contacts or wiring! So if you read more than about 10 mV across the closed contacts of the thermostat, look out! Go to the thermostat itself, take the cover off, and read the contact resistance. If it is very low, short the two leads together, go back to the control unit, disconnect the leads, and see if you get more than 1-2 ohms across the wires. If you do, there is probably a twisted splice somewhere in the wiring!

Contacts on the thermostat itself can be cleaned with a piece of plain paper. As a rule, never use emery paper on contacts in a millivoltage system. If they're so bad that they have too much resistance, replace the thermostat. The same test can be used on the limit switch, which is exactly the same as the thermostat, but works at different temperatures.

Quick Checks

One good quick-check for thermostat, limit switch, or wiring trouble is to jumper contacts on the control unit. If this lets the main burner come on normally, you have located the cause of the trouble. Same old process of elimination used in all electrical and electronic troubleshooting. Do not leave jumpers in place across safety devices such as limit switches, etc!

After the process of elimination, you will have the faulty part pinned down. Replace the defective parts and recheck. The thermostat, limit switch, and thermocouple are fairly easy to replace, if directions (always packed with the new unit) are followed. If all of the other things are working, but the main burner refuses to come on, the valve itself is defective.

CAUTION! The valve can sometimes be taken apart and cleaned or replaced. This job should be handled by a licensed gas plumber. Do-it-yourselfing here could lead to danger, unless you are an experienced pipefitter, and take every precaution to check out the whole system for gas leaks! Use soap bubbles and a small brush. Even at these low pressures, any gas leakage is potentially very dangerous! However, the electrical parts of the system can be checked by any competent technician, once he knows what the normal reactions are, and this is what we've tried to give you here.

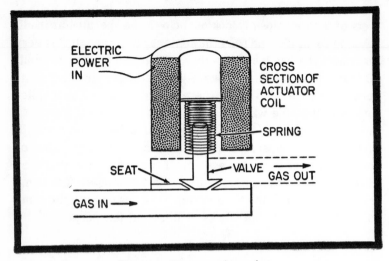

Fig. 5-3. Gas or water valve.

The basic design of an electrical valve includes some sort of spring-loaded actuator. The spring holds the valve mechanism in the off or closed position; when power is applied, the actuating coil pulls a plunger up, which opens the valve. Figure 5-3 shows the schematic of this kind of unit. The spring forces the valve itself into the seal, keeping it closed. The valve itself may be of brass or any other material, but the upper part, the cylinder, will be made of soft iron. So, when electrical power is applied to the actuating coil, this rod is lifted or pulled into the coil, opening the valve. This is called a "solenoid" (and some day I'm going to look up the origin of that word).

As long as everything is copacetic normal operating power applied, the valve stays open. If the power fails, or if the regular turnoff switch opens (control thermostat, etc.), the spring pushes the valve shut, quickly and positively. This basic action leads to a distinct resemblance between all types of these valves, whether they control gas, water, oil, or anything else.

The operating voltage will vary, of course. Some work on 117V (or even 240V), others work on 24V(from a small transformer), and some even work on the very minute dc voltages developed by a thermocouple. This will give us different values for test readings, but we can always use the same basic check; apply normal operating power to the thing and see if it works!

For a general rule, if we can read the normal operating voltage across the coil terminals, but the valve will not open, it's defective. In most cases, you'll hear a little click or thump when the valve operates. If the control has been taken off, for testing, you can blow into the input connections, then apply power and see if it opens.

If the coil is open, it will show up on an ohmmeter test. The resistance of the coils will vary. The higher the operating voltage, the lower the coil resistance. Some of the millivolt-system coils will have a pretty high resistance—they need quite a few turns of fine wire to develop a usable magnetic field from such a little supply. By the way, in some of the millivolt systems, you'll find coils that are not intended to pull the valve open. When the thermocouple heats up, it will develop enough power to hold the valve open, but you will have to push a lever, etc. to open it manually. Others are designed to pull the valve open often with a bleeder diaphragm. The gas pressure helps to open the valve.

If the coil checks good, but the valve will not open, there's a good possibility that the actuating rod in the solenoid is being bound or jammed by dirt, foreign matter, etc. that has gotten into the valve from the gas or water supply. A great many of these can be taken apart and cleaned without too much trouble. Figure 5-4 shows a typical direct-operated valve of this type. The coil and working parts will be enclosed in a housing, held in place by screws. If you take one of these apart, remember where everything goes, and in what order!

Any dirt that is jamming the operating parts of the valve can be cleaned out. Polish tightly fitting parts, such as rods, until they're very smooth and shiny. If the valve was leaking, check the valve and seat for small particles of dirt which is keeping the valve from seating tightly.

As a general rule, you shouldn't use too much lubricant on these things. If any, use one of the silicone oils or greases.

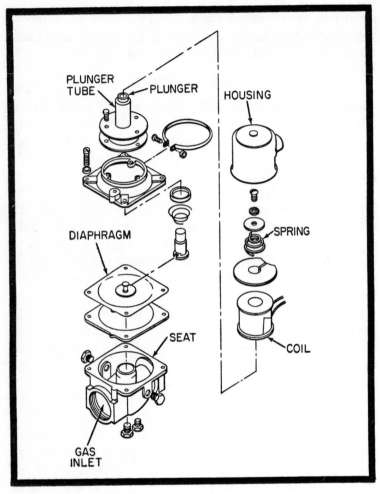

Fig. 5-4. Direct-operated valve (exploded view).

There is also a spray-can product, available from refrigeration-supply houses, which actually leaves a very thin film of Teflon on the surfaces!

Never use excessive oil or grease. It will tend to make the valve jam sooner than it should. Apply it very sparingly if at all.

When you get it back together, check it very carefully for quick, positive shutoff, and full opening.

40

Grounds and Safety

We hear a lot about safety and "consumerism" these days. This is nothing new! This is just the same old "customer relations" that we've all worked on so hard for the past many years. They're just making more noise about it lately. Safety, of course, is what those of us who are still here have been observing all along! However, they have come up with some new ideas, and some of them are pretty darn good; especially those that really protect.

A great many appliances have metal cases, trim, and so on. So it is easy to see that a short or leakage from the ac line to the case could do one of two things—make the whole case hot to any grounded object, or ground it. A 50-50 chance, depending on where the short is and how the thing is plugged in. These aren't nearly good enough odds for the protection of our customers! Since "any grounded object" includes such things as sink faucets and even cement floors when they're a little damp, we've got a very dangerous situation. So, let's do something about it.

They're using a system which will give us positive protection against internal electrical leakages and shorts. This is the "third wire," a separate pin on the electrical plug which does nothing but ground the case of the appliance. The diagram of Fig. 6-1 shows one of these.

Let's look at some figures that will shock you (and perhaps keep some of your customers from a different kind). Even a very minute leakage from a hot wire inside an appliance, to the metal case, can cause a shock hazard.

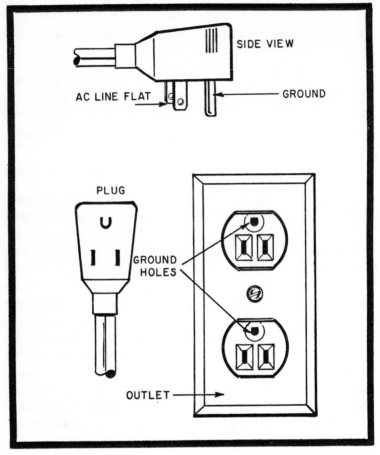

SIDE VIEW

AC LINE FLAT

GROUND

PLUG

GROUND HOLES

OUTLET

Fig. 6-1. Three-wire plug and receptacle.

The housewife who is using these appliances isn't a professional. She is almost certain to touch an appliance with one hand and a faucet with the other. To make it worse, her hands are very apt to be damp!

This is the best possible condition for a severe shock. Damp skin has very low resistance. Also, the "circuit" is the most dangerous one you can find; up one arm, across the chest (and through the heart) and down the other arm. If the victim's hands happen to be closed around the object, she can't let go. Her muscles contract, and she grips the thing more tightly (reducing the resistance even more)! The breathing control centers become paralyzed and that's it. Fibrillation of the heart sets in, and it's death from shock!

So it's up to us, as professional workers in either electronics or electrical wiring, to make sure that these safety devices are safe and properly connected. They should be checked every time anything electrical is serviced. This doesn't take long. A quick ohmmeter check between the third pin of the plug and the case, which should show zero ohms, and a check from both of the line pins to the case, which should show infinity.

Since a three-wire plug arrangement is polarized, there is theoretically no way to plug it into a three-wire socket except the way it was intended to be plugged in—unless the third pin is defeated or cut off. Inside the convenience outlet, you'll find that the ground-pin receptacle is connected to the conduit along with one of the other two wires. Thus, there is really no problem if one of the two flat prongs of an appliance shows a resistance of zero ohms to the appliance case, so long as the appliance is not used with an extension cord (i.e., so long as the purpose of the polarizing plug is not defeated or cheated in any way).

As an appliance safety doublecheck, plug it in and take an ac voltage reading between the case and a known ground. It should show absolutely zero voltage, of course. If you do get even a very small voltage, find out why. This can come from odd things. An accumulation of lint and dust making a conductive bridge from a hot terminal to the case, especially in damp environments, and so on. Of course, there is always a chance of a careless repair job in the past, leaving strands of wire touching the case.

The "third wire" is the best safety feature of all. By making the exposed metal case of the unit ground at all times, any electrical leakage will have a path to ground. If the leakage is high enough, it will trip the circuit breaker or blow the fuse. That's what it's supposed to do! If it is correctly hooked up, the appliance will never become a "third rail."

Just to make sure, it's not a bad idea to check this in houses where the outlets are all of the three-wire type. Use a standard electrician's test lamp. The incandescent test lamp should light to full brilliance between the hot terminal of the receptacle and the round hole or ground. If it does not, if it lights only dimly, this means that the protective grounding is bad! If you find this, let your customer know about it and tell him he must have it checked by an electrician at once.

There is another matter concerning safety, but not so much for the consumer as for you, yourself. It has to do with wire coding, where black is white and white is black! I had another little saying for this, which was even more confusing! "**Black is hot, and white is not, and vice is often versa!**" This has nothing to do with integration or anything like that. It refers to a squabble that's been going on between electronics men and electricians for a long time. Since it is something we both run into every day, I thought it might be a good idea to "issue a reminder" about it.

It has to do with the color-coding of wires. Electronics men think of black wires as always being ground. White wires are always "hot," in the sense of being at a potential above ground. (Actually, the code for a white wire means that it is the centertap of an i-f transformer.)

Electricians use an entirely different coding, and it is a standard code, by the way. If I'm not mistaken, this is from the NEC (National Electrical Code). For all 120 | 240-volt systems of home and industrial wiring, the black wire is always hot, and the white wire is always ground (or "neutral"). So there is the possibility of confusion for both of us, if we get into the other's territory. This is most important where dangerous voltages exist.

There has been a lot of uproar lately about safety, proper grounding, and so on. So if we (electronics men) get into any household wiring problems, we must remember which wire is which! Don't ever reach into a box and grab a black wire, secure in the conviction that "black is always ground." It isn't! (You'll find out as soon as you come to.)

In the three-wire 240-volt services found in many homes today, you'll find a three-wire cable. This is used for many large appliances—clothes dryers, water heaters, and so on. Once again, the white wire is the ground or neutral, the black wire is one of the hot ones, and the remaining wire is probably red, also hot (and now they're getting back to our code, where red wires are always hot!). The diagram of Fig. 6-2 shows the voltages and colors used.

This is a single-phase 240V system. You get the full 240V between the two colored conductors, and 120V between either of the colored conductors and the white or ground wire. Appliances using 240V are connected to the colored wires only, and all of the 120V loads are connected to one or the other colored wire and the white wire as a common. (This is exactly the same as our familiar power supply transformer with a

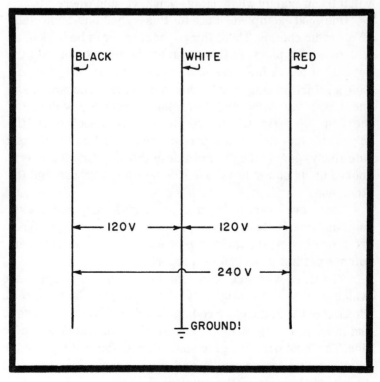

Fig. 6-2. Three-wire household power.

centertapped secondary. Of course, the transformer, out on the pole, is about 3 feet bigger!)

So when you hook up any appliance that requires a ground, check the connections to the electrical outlet, and connect the ground to the terminal with the white wire. You might run into this if the unit has a polarized plug, or one of the later plugs— the one with the two flat pins and a third, round pin, which is always ground. Incidentally, in the line cord to the appliance, this third wire is coded green.

Don't be overconfident. Just as in lots of electronics gear, you'll find cases where the maker did NOT use standard color-coding, or where some inexperienced electrician hooked up the wire colors incorrectly! (I could show you some wiring like that in my own home; installed a long, long time ago!) So, for safety's sake, TEST! Use a neon test lamp and a known ground such as a cold-water pipe. This, plus an ac voltmeter, will tell you exactly what voltage you have, and where.

One good example of a use for this is the "line-connected" TV or radio chassis. These things should always be hooked up with polarized plugs, so that it cannot be plugged in with the hot side of the ac line connected to the chassis. If it does not have a polarized plug, and far too many of them do not, install one. Check the outlet, and if necessary replace it with one of the new 3-pin types. The circuit can be checked on the schematic, and the new line cord connected so that the chassis side always goes to the ground side of the line. (In all properly hooked up ac power lines, one side is always ground and the other hot.)

There are several types of polarized plug and socket combinations for 120V service. However, the new 3-pin types are much better, for there is no way that you can use them without getting it hooked up properly.

The three-wire line cords can be added to any appliance which didn't have it originally. When you do this, be sure to check it out with the color coding. Black and white wires go to the motor, heating element, or anything connected to the ac line. The third wire, the green one, goes to the round pin of the plug ("round for ground") and must always be connected tightly to the case of the appliance!

Photocircuits: Light-Operated Control

You're going to run into several kinds of appliances which are turned on or off automatically by the presence or absence of light. Not too far back, this would have meant a vacuum-tube photocell, an amplifier, dc power supply, relay, and a pretty bulky "package" of electronics. They're getting a lot smaller. There is a solid-state device that can be turned on or off by light, and guess what? It's our old friend the SCR in a new version: one single SCR in a discrete package with a hole in the top, and actuated by light. This is the LASCR.

These are just like phototransistors. Actually, all transistor junctions are photosensitive—light falling on 'em makes 'em turn on. All they have to do to make a phototransistor is leave a hole in the top of the case so light can hit the junctions. The LASCR can be turned on by light falling on it. In other words: with light, conduction; no light, no conduction.

There are applications where we need full-wave conduction. So, we have to use a "double SCR" or triac, since the basic SCR cuts off half of the applied ac, like any diode. Also, in a lot of cases, we need an "opposite reaction": turn on when there is no light, turn off when there is. So we add a few little gubbins to the circuit, like the one shown in Fig. 7-1, from RCA's "Solid-State Controls" book, and there we are.

The circuit shown doesn't use LASCRs, by the way. It doesn't even use light-activated triacs! The circuit shown uses a conventional triac, a conventional diac, and a photocell whose resistance changes according to the amount of light falling on its surface. In the circuit, we've drawn the diac the way RCA does—like a triac without a gate. In most texts,

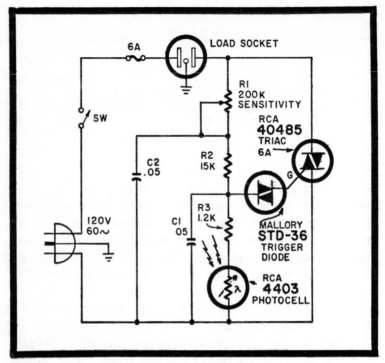

Fig. 7-1. Light-operated circuit.

you'll find the diac drawn as a baseless npn transistor whose collector has an outward-going arrowhead to match that of the "emitter" (see Fig. 2-6).

What Are They Used For?

There are lots of applications for this kind of thing; automatic yard lights that turn on at sunset; automatic night lights, room lights, garage door openers, and so on and on. Three resistors, two capacitors, and three solid-state devices—and there you are. The RCA 40485 is a 6-amp triac, so it will handle up to 700 watts or so. There are higher-rated types if needed.

How Does It Work?

When there is no light falling on the photocell, its resistance is high. So the ac voltage coming through sensitivity control R1 and resistor R2 can charge capacitor C1 to a high voltage, twice during each full cycle. This builds up enough voltage to fire the trigger diode, which in turn fires the triac and discharges the capacitor. This is the on condition; whatever load is plugged into the load socket will be energized.

In a yard light, this would be "night"; no ambient light, so the light turns on. When day breaks, the light increases (unless the smog is too thick). The increased light falling on the photocell makes its resistance drop. Since the photoelectric cell is actually shunted across C1, it prevents the voltage on the capacitor from rising to a level high enough to fire the diac; so the triac won't fire either, and the light goes off.

This circuit, as is, would be all you'd need for an automatic yard light. It could also be used for things such as counting packages on a conveyor belt, counting people going through a gate to a sporting event, etc.

With an external relay plugged into the load socket, it could be used to start or stop a motor.

This circuit could be "reversed"; made to turn lights on when light hits the photoelectric cell (automatic garage lights which turn on when the car's headlights hit the cell, or even a garage door opener which works when the headlights shine on it, etc.).

If anything goes wrong, servicing is simple. Any of these things can be checked out with an ohmmeter and an ac voltmeter. Just like checking transistors. Look for a short or open. If C1 is shorted, you won't be able to get enough gate voltage on the trigger diode. So, the thing would stay off at all times. If C1 was open or leaky, the chances are that it would either refuse to work or operate erratically. If either the diac or the triac shorts, the light will stay on all the time.

The photocell causes little trouble; if you suspect it, check it with an ohmmeter. Dark, it should have a very high resistance. Shine a flashlight on it and the resistance should go way down. If it'll do this, it's all right.

When Wiring Acts Up

A lot of the time, the simple things cause all the trouble. What could be simpler than the wiring in a typical appliance? Yet, this is a very important part of it—in two or three different ways, as we shall see.

Wires are more than long skinny hunks of copper connected between things. Modern wiring has several special characteristics. If we know these and what to do with them, we can save a lot of trouble.

When does a piece of wire need replacing? When you can bend it and see the insulation crack. Worse, when you can move it, and the insulation falls off in your hand. (Also, of course, when your ohmmeter shows no continuity, but this is pretty obvious.)

Don't tape up bad places in the insulation! This is a real no-no. Why? Because if the insulation has gone bad where you can see it, the chances are it has also gone bad at some place where you can't. And there's always the chance of the tape baking out and going bad in turn. Now, what kind of wire to use for a replacement? That's a good question—let's see if we can find a good answer.

WIRE SIZES

The most important thing is to use wire big enough to handle the current. Table 8-1 shows the ratings for common wire-gage standards. Check the maximum current, given on the rating plate. In the figure for wattage, move the decimal two places left to determine approximate amperage.

If the wire is fixed, and doesn't have to bend, solid wire is best. If it must be bent or flexed, stranded wire is necessary.

The more flexibility needed, the greater the number of strands you should use. For example, for "moderate flexing" of a No. 14 wire, the recommendation is for a 65 x 30 (65 strands of No. 30). For "service" flexing, 165 x 34; 165 strands of No. 34, and so on.

Table 8-1. Current Capacity of Flexible Wire

AWG	*Rubber and Plastic Wire	*Heater Wire	
18	10	10	*Ampere ratings for UL and NEC
17	11 (SVT)	12	standard 2-conductor and 3-
	12 (SVHT)		conductor (2-circuit con-
16	13	15	ductors) wire. Wire with 4 to 6
14	18	20	conductors or 3 or more circuit
12	25	30	conductors have lower current
10	30	—	ratings. No. 27 AWG tinsel cor-
8	40	—	dage rates 0.5 amp.
6	55	—	
4	70	—	

INSULATION

All insulation used was rubber, a while ago. That's all changed now. We have a great many modern materials, in the various plastics. Rubber was good while it lasted, and you can take that either way. It did have a tendency to get brittle with age. High heat, especially in the presence of ozone, ages rubber much more rapidly. So practically all of the new wire you get will have plastic insulation.

The most common will probably be the vinyls and the polyethylenes. They are thermoplastics. They melt easily. Except in very special uses, they are the ones you'll see. The others are thermosetting plastics. This includes rubber, by the way! The new ones are Neoprene, and some of the silicone plastics. These are molded by heat, then they set, and can't be remelted.

The big difference lies in the maximum temperature that each type can withstand. If it gets too hot, many of the thermoplastics will melt and fall off the wires! For a rule of thumb, plain rubber wire can be used in places where the temperature will not exceed 60°C (about 132°F). The vinyls and polyethylenes are rated in the same area. If we must go

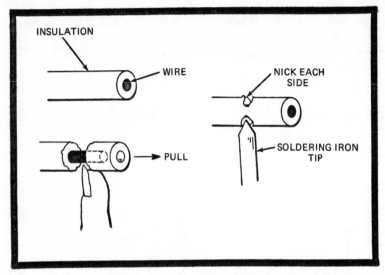

Fig. 8-1. Removing wire insulation with solder-iron heat.

above this, to about 90°C, we'll need Neoprene insulation. In fact, UL allows the use of a jacketed Neoprene wire up to 105°C. Above that, a silicone-insulated, fiber-glass jacketed wire is needed. A new Dupont plastic, "Hypalon" (chlorosulfonated polyethylene for short), is now coming into use for temperatures up to 130°C.

The old standby for hot wires—asbestos—is still with us. You'll find it used in flexible cords for electric irons and other high-current appliances. Asbestos-covered wire is fine, but it, too, has limitations. In a lot of cases, it will be simply laid up around the wire. This needs a stout braid jacket, mainly to keep the asbestos in place! Don't use asbestos wire with laid insulation in places where it must flex or where it can touch the metal case of the unit. This insulation can be pulled off the wire with your fingers!

Another thing we must beware of is crush. In many appliances, especially smaller, hand-held types, the wiring runs in slots or grooves inside two-piece metal handles, cases, and so on. Unless we are very careful putting the thing back together, the wires can be caught between two sharp metal edges. When the bolts are tightened, these can crush the insulation. This could cause a short to the case. Even if the insulation is not crushed when the case is first tightened, it could be softened by heat later on as the unit is used, and then short!

INSTALLATION

When we install new wires, they must be handled and worked with the correct methods. This is especially important in some of the things using very small wires.

In the past, most of us grabbed the end of the wire between the jaws of our diagonals and yanked, pulling the insulation off.

Modern plastics are pretty tough. If the wire inside is very small, you can break it before you pull the insulation off! And, of course, the break will be somewhere inside an apparently undamaged part of the insulation.

There's a very easy way. Just touch the tip of a soldering iron to each side of the insulation, where you want it pulled off. Figure 8-1 shows how. Melt a tiny nick in each side, then pull the insulation off with a thumbnail. Using this method, you won't run the chance of cutting or breaking several of the tiny strands of the wire! Better still, use the proper wirestripper.

Watch it when making solder joints with this type of wire! Whenever possible, do not solder a thermoplastic insulated wire, if it is leaving the terminal in a sharp bend, as in Fig. 8-2A. The wire carries the heat very nicely, softens the insulation, which promptly straightens out, leaving you with about an inch of nice bare wire (Fig. 8-2B).

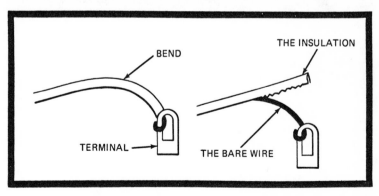

Fig. 8-2. Soldering solid wire to terminals.

To avoid this, be sure the wire is straight. A better way is to heatsink it. Grab the wire between the tips of a pair of long-nose pliers, as close to the solder joint as you can get. It will also help to tin the stranded wires before starting. Hold the wire between the jaw tips, and quickly tin it with fresh solder. Now, you won't have to stay on the joint so long to get a good scald on it. Heatsink it with the pliers anyhow; it couldn't hurt.

For a final word, study the characteristics of each type of wire. If you know what it can do, and, much more important, what it can't do, you will find things a lot easier! Use the right wire in the right place.

DC Small-Appliance Motors 9

Not too long ago I ran across an interesting application of electronic equipment in home appliances (by special request). The request was "Daddy! My styling comb won't work!"For those unfamiliar with this latest fruit of our technology, it's a little hand-held gizmo like a hair dryer. It has a heating element and a fan. These are built into a small handle. A special comb or brush can be plugged into the warm air outlet. Long hair can be blown dry as it is combed out.

Dissecting this little monster with some difficulty, I found a miniature motor with a plastic fan, a heating element, and a blob. Three wires came out of the blob, which was tightly wrapped with glass fiber tape. These wires went to the heating element and the motor. Since the thing is powered by ac, I expected an ac motor.

However, the heating element heated, but the motor declined to operate. Out of the case it came, after more difficulty in locating a subminiature Phillips screwdriver. I expected the motor to be open. So some circuit-tracing was in order.

The heating element was tapped. Hmm. What for? Spreading it out on the bench, I drew out a circuit diagram (Fig. 9-1).

Rearranging the crude first draft of the schematic, I could see what was going on. Evidently they were taking a low ac voltage off the taps on the heating element, applying them to the blob, which had to be a rectifier, and running the motor on dc! Now that I took a closer look at it, this looked exactly like some of the mini-motors used to run toys, etc. Unhooking the

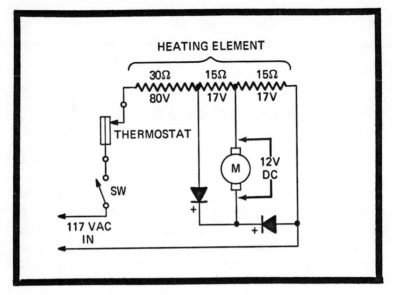

Fig. 9-1. Electric styling comb schematic.

leads to the motor, I connected them to the bench variable dc power supply. The motor would run at only 3V, and at 10V it really turned up revs.

Checking out the blob, I could see markings plainly (Fig. 9-2). There were two symbols which indicated ac on the outer leads, so the center lead had to be a common. A little fast work with the ohmmeter confirmed this. On one side, at least. The other one was shorted. From the polarity of the surviving diode, the thing was a common-cathode full-wave rectifier. Now I needed a replacement.

Turning the heating element on again, I read 15V ac on either side of the centertap. So peak voltage wouldn't be any problem. Current wouldn't be either. This little motor probably took about 1 ampere maximum. Picking up a pair of standard silicon diodes from the TV replacement stock, I haywired them together, and hooked them up with clip-leads. Firing it up, the motor ran very nicely! I read 12V dc across the motor.

By clipping the leads of the diodes very short and making careful lap joints, which I covered with short pieces of spaghetti, I rewrapped the original tape and came out with a "package" that was actually a bit smaller than the original.

One unexpected problem cropped up. While testing, I'd had the whole thing propped up on a plastic box to clear the fan. When I began to put it back together, I discovered that the delicate heating element was firmly stuck to the plastic! Answer? Simple. Turn the thing on again. When the element heated up, it came out of the plastic.

We will probably see quite a few similar applications of this, in the smaller hand-held appliances. The circuit is simple, but ingenious. The tiny motors won't carry too much load, but in uses such as this, they don't have to. This one had only a small fan, which it turned with ease. Slightly larger motors and bigger rectifiers, and larger loads could be handled without trouble.

This could be done in several ways. One likely prospect would be small SCRs that vary the ac voltage applied to the rectifiers; or, variable resistors, or any one of several other ways. While checking this one, I noted that the motor speed seemed to be proportional to the applied dc voltage.

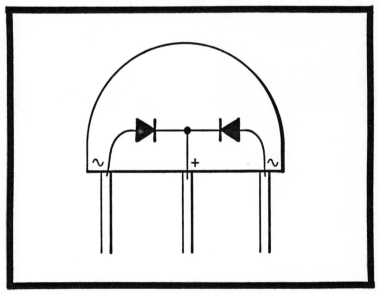

Fig. 9-2. Rectifier module in styling comb.

If you open up this type of appliance with motor troubles, and find a little three-legged blob, unwrap it and see if it isn't a rectifier. If so, it can be replaced with ease. The stock silicon diodes we use for TV power supply replacements have ample peak voltage ratings, and they can be bought with current ratings up to 2 amperes for a very nominal sum. Incidentally, encapsulated full-wave rectifiers just like the blob are available from any of several semiconductor makers. I just didn't happen to have one on hand.

Electrical Interference

Formula for a domestic catastrophe: Dad in the living room watching the evening news. Mom in kitchen decides to make up a batch of slaw in the blender. Or daughter decides to dry her hair with her new dryer. Or son decides to finish his hair-do. Result: machinery starts, and there is a loud roar, "Turn that thing off! It's tearin' up my TV!"

In other words, one of these useful household gadgets has decided to become a miniature broadcasting station, radiating assorted rf interference like mad. Let's see what to do about it, to restore peace to the home.

Practically all appliances that cause TVI (television interference) use small, high-torque brush-type motors. A few use buzzer-type contacts. Either of these cause tiny arcs, and the resulting hash contains noise components in every common frequency band—AM, FM, TV, you name it.

There are two ways of reducing or eliminating this noise. The first is to reduce the amplitude of the arcing at brushes or contacts. Clean up the commutator if it is dark and pitted. Check the brushes for length; if they're worn so that the springs do not have enough tension to hold them tightly against the commutator, the arcing is much worse. The end of a good brush is smooth and shiny.

A commutator can be cleaned, if you can get at it, by cutting a thin strip of fine sandpaper, wrapping it over the end of a small stick, and holding it against the commutator while it's running. DON'T use emery cloth. The abrasive material is conductive, and will get into the motor. For most small motors, the standard "nail-boards" (sandpaper coating on stiff cardboard, available in the manicure section of

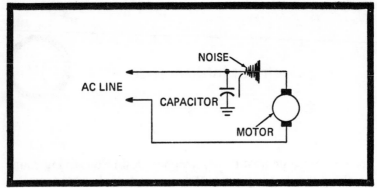

Fig. 10-1. Filtering of hash.

drugstores) are very handy. They can be cut into thin strips, small enough to get into even very small commutators. Check to see that the brushes are not sticking in their holders and be sure that the springs have enough tension. If brushes bounce, this makes the arcing worse. If you can't reduce the arcing, and you see the "ring of fire" all the way around the commutator as it runs, the armature is apt to be defective. The only cure is to replace the motor.

The second method is filtering. This means providing an easy path for the noise to get to ground, or keep it inside the case of the unit. Figure 10-1 shows the general idea. This noise is mostly very high frequency hash. We make use of the basic property of a capacitor—it will pass ac but block dc and low frequencies. So we connect a bypass capacitor from the noise-source to a ground. This provides a very low-impedance path for the noise, but has no perceptible effect on the 60 Hz ac line voltage.

In older appliances, with metal cases, the filter capacitor can be connected from the brush to the frame of the motor. One capacitor should be connected from each brush to the frame. If the unit has one of the 3-wire line cords, with the separate external ground lead (the green one), filters could be connected from the brush to this wire, which is an external ground.

In the bigger units, space won't be too much of a problem. You'll be able to put the filter capacitors on the end of the motor and tuck them away tightly. In some of the more compact types with plastic cases, you won't have too much room. However, you can get disc capacitors up to 0.05 uF that are small enough to tuck away inside the smaller cases. Be sure to insulate the leads well. Use a good grade of braid or spaghetti (NOT a thermoplastic tubing, that will melt if the case gets too hot).

For 117V circuits, use capacitors with a minimum voltage rating of 200 volts (600V types are better if you can get them in). For subminiature types, using dc motors and low voltages, even the little transistor-type capacitors can be used. Use whatever value cuts down the noise the most.

If the filter capacitors won't cut the interference to a suitable level, you may have to try small rf chokes in series with the motor leads. These can be handwound (air-core) from solid wire. Cover them with tape and tuck them away in the case.

If there isn't room for anything like this, you may have to use an external filter. Figure 10-2 shows a typical circuit for one of these. If there is room inside the appliance case, this works better at that point. If not, you can build it, and connect it in series with the ac line. There are several different types and makes of these, made with a plug and socket, so that they

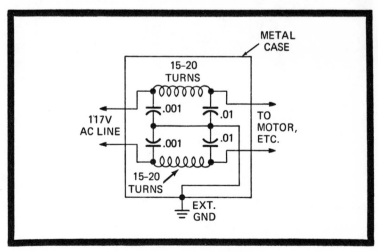

Fig. 10-2. Homebrew rf filter.

can be plugged into the outlet, and the appliance line cord plugged into the filter. Some of these have an external ground terminal on the side of the case. In severe cases, this will often help a good deal.

Run a short lead to a cold-water pipe, etc.

If you want to make up one of these, put it in a small metal case and make the case the external ground terminal. Do not try to use the "line ground" or white wire. Keep both ac line conductors well insulated from the case of the filter. Use terminal strips, etc. to support the connections.

The basic principle of all noise filtering, of course, is to keep the noise inside the apparatus generating it. Once it gets out onto the line-cord, you have it on a pretty darned efficient antenna for radiating it.

The Ground-Fault Interrupter

There is a new safety device on the market. Not new, in the sense of having just been invented, but certainly not commonly known. It is the "ground-fault interrupter." For a test, I asked several electricians what it was, and the majority answer was "Huh?"

One power company engineer told me that he had one at the substation. True, they have been used for quite a while there, in heavy-duty types. (Another one said "Ground-fault interrupter? Some kind of electronic thing to prevent earthquakes?" I told him that the San Andreas fault was not the kind of ground fault I meant!) Seriously speaking, this device is not well known yet, although the 1971 National Electrical Code specifies its use in certain locations!

The ground-fault interrupter (or GFI) is a dual-purpose, very sensitive, extremely fast-acting circuit breaker. It provides the same overcurrent protection as the regular circuit breakers. In addition, it can sense very minute ground currents. These are currents which flow whenever a leakage or short to ground occurs—for one example, a person touching the hot wire while standing on a grounded surface.

A conventional circuit breaker, of course, will not open the circuit when this type of fault occurs. A GFI will. Not only this, it will do it so fast that it can save the person from electrocution! Let's see how this is done. A bit of history first.

GFIs have been in use in power stations for a long time. They trip at 20-40 amperes, which is okay for that kind of service. Smaller, more sensitive units were developed and used in Europe several years ago. However, by U.S. standards, these were considered marginal in both speed and current limiting. So, we went to work to make them faster and safer.

As many experiments have established, it may take as little as 20 milliamperes of current through the human body to cause ventricular fibrillation of the heart (interruption of its normal rhythm, so that it flutters wildly instead of beating). This is measured through the most likely path (arm to leg) so that the shock currents pass through the chest region. This is also very close to the "let-go" threshold—the current value above which the muscles contract and you can't let go of the wire. You freeze to it, and without protection, you have had it!

This was the objection to the French and Austrian versions of the GFI. Their trip value was up around 30 mA, considered to be far too high for maximum protection. So, U.S. engineers went to work to speed it up, and they did. Typical ratings for production GFIs are now down to a sensitivity of 5.0 mA, and the tip time has been reduced to 0.025 second! That's 25 milliseconds.

To clear up one point before we go any farther, the GFI does not limit the current that can flow through the fault. It limits the time during which it can flow. So the total energy fed through the fault (human body, or whatever else) is limited by limiting the pulse width.

Now, how does it do this? The GFI contains standard circuit breakers that will open if the load current exceeds their trip ratings. These are electrically operated by a coil— something like the large "contactors" used in industrial electrical work. A fault current energizes the coil and opens the circuit very quickly. This refers to the normal load current flowing in the circuit.

Beside these, the GFI contains a sensing circuit that can detect very small currents flowing from the line to ground. Normal load currents flow up one side and down the other. If we have 2.0 amperes going one way in wire A, we'd have the same going the other way in wire B. The circuit is balanced. To verify this, take the standard clamp-on ac ammeter, and hook it around only one wire—you get a reading. The same with the other wire. Now hook it around both wires at once—no reading, because the line is balanced.

That's how the GFI gets its information as to when to trip! The two (or three) "circuit wires" are run through a differential transformer. A sensor winding on the toroidal core is the key to the whole process. As long as only normal currents flow in the circuit, no voltage is induced in this winding.

When there is a ground fault from either of the hot wires to earth, current flows. It creates an imbalance and a voltage is induced in the sensor winding. This causes the sensor unit to energize the trip coil (it uses the power from the line to do this) and open the hot sides of the circuit.

Commercial units, such as those made by the Harvey Hubbell Co. of Bridgeport, Conn., have overcurrent ratings of 15 and 20 amperes, sensitivity of 5.0 mA fault-current, and a trip-time of 0.025 second. These units use the differential-transformer sensor, and the glass-enclosed reed switches for the actual tripping of the coils. There are other companies making these units, too. Some are standard box mountings for home use. There is also a portable unit, with an extension cord, for the protection of workmen, handymen, and any use where there is danger of shock from electric tools or equipment.

They are required by the NFPA Code for all electrical outlets within 15 feet of swimming pools. Later on, this could be extended to other areas of the home where dampness and electrical equipment meet—laundry rooms, and even kitchens or baths.

There are complications, of course. If you should install one of these devices, only to find that it trips instantly, stop. You have very likely got some leakage in your wiring! Older houses, water-soaked conduit wiring, faulty appliances, etc. will trip the GFI. This is an indication of a hazardous condition and it had better be found and fixed! In January 1969 the National Standards Institute issued a new Standard for leakage current in appliances. This allowed 0.5 mA or less of leakage in all cord-connected units. If you have a leakage greater than the 5 mA trip current of the GFI, it won't stay in, but it's trying to tell you something!

These things are not cheap; that is, compared to the cost of the older overcurrent protection devices like circuit breakers. However, when you think of what they could save— this includes your life and your children's lives—they are! They will protect against possible lethal shocks, and this is pretty much priceless!

Solid-State Speed Controls

Several home appliances use multiple-speed control systems. Most common would probably be the food mixer, or blender. There are some with "continuously variable" speed-controls. Those will be dealt with later. More common are "step" systems; a button is pushed, and the motor runs at the desired speed until switched off.

The original system used a mechanical governor. It had a pair of contacts on the end of the armature shaft, actuated by weights. It was called a "centrifugal governor" because it was actuated by centrifugal force. When the motor reached the desired speed, the contacts opened, breaking the supply circuit. They stayed open until the armature slowed down. Then they closed, applying power again. The action is very rapid.

This method has a couple of disadvantages. For one, the contacts arced, and eventually got very dirty. Also, the arcing generated a healthy amount of TVI and RFI, upsetting any radio or TV in the vicinity!

Solid-state controls offer the same flexibility, but without the disadvantages of noise and possible bad contacts. One of these uses a tapped motor winding, as shown in Fig. 12-1, with an 8-position speed-selector switch. The motors used in this type must always be the "universal" (ac-dc) type.

For the highest speed, the ac line is connected directly to the full winding. The next three taps are lower speeds, with full-wave ac fed to the motor. From here on, the same four taps on the winding are used, but now a diode is connected in series with each one. So the motor gets half-wave-rectified dc, with less than half the power. These diodes are often "encapsulated" in a single block, although they can be separate units.

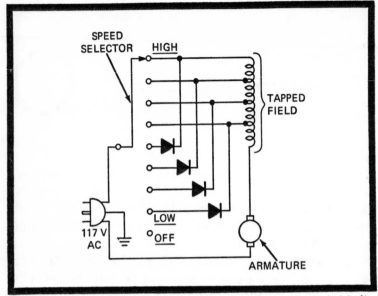

Fig. 12-1. Four taps on winding are followed by diodes connected to the same taps, giving the mixer an 8-position speed control.

Checking this kind of speed control can be simple. Only an ac voltmeter and ohmmeter are needed. If you have trouble on the higher speeds, check the selector switch and the motor windings for continuity. For instance, if the motor will not run on the two highest-speed positions, but will run normally from "there on down," you have an open motor winding or selector switch (most probably the switch). If it will run on positions 3 and 4, and 7 and 8, but not on 1-2 or 5-6, this would point to the upper taps on the motor as the cause.

If the motor runs on high speeds, and switches to lower speeds, but suddenly jumps back to full speed, say on position 7, the chances are that the diode in that position is shorted. If it runs on all other positions but stops on 7, the diode, or that switch contact, would be open. The ohmmeter will tell you which one it is. If you read the full ac line voltage on the input to the diode, but the motor won't run, there you are: open diode.

Figure 12-2 shows another type of speed control. This one uses an SCR; the motor, of course, must be designed to reach

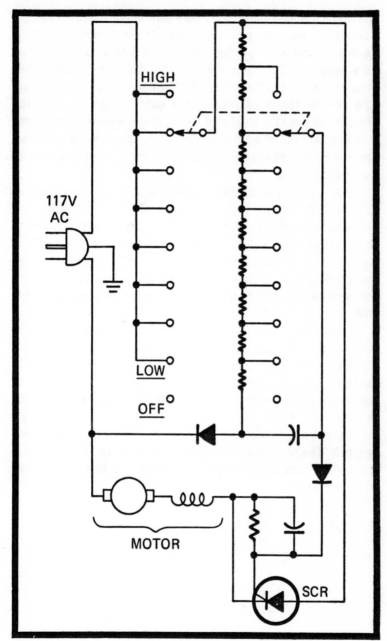

Fig. 12-2. SCR controls speed of motor. Gate voltage of SCR is controlled by a switch and resistors. This type has speed regulation.

the highest speed needed on only half-wave rectified dc. An 8-position, two-deck selector switch is used, just as before. (Actually, the main purpose of the left side is to provide an OFF position!) The right side does the "business"; it switches taps on a voltage driver network to control the SCR gating. The greater the resistance in the gate voltage divider, the shorter the time the SCR will be on, and the slower the motor will run. Unlike the type in Fig. 12-1, this circuit provides speed control and speed regulation, with the RC networks and extra diodes, etc.

Once again, testing can be quite easy. If the motor runs at full speed at all times, the motor and SCR are all right. The chances are that the selector switch or one of the resistors in the gate voltage divider, or both, would be open. If the SCR is shorted, the chances are that the motor would run at a speed much faster than normal, since it would then have full-power full-wave ac applied to it. The SCR can be checked for shorts with an ohmmeter.

Incidentally, you should be able to make a substitution test for a suspected SCR; just unhook it and temporarily connect a standard silicon rectifier (with sufficient current capacity, of course!) into the circuit in its place. If the motor will run at full speed, the motor itself is okay and you've got trouble in the SCR, switch, etc.

Here again, you may run into encapsulated or "black box" controls. The tests described can be made on the motor, and if these show that it is in working order, the entire control unit must be replaced.

Is The Ground Grounded Or Ungrounded

The National Electrical Code (NEC for short) for 1971 specifies "All interior wiring systems shall have a grounded conductor which is continuously indentified throughout the system" (except for certain specialized cases like hospital operating rooms, etc. where an intentionally ungrounded system is used). Also, "Identification of grounded conductors shall be as follows:—shall have an outer identification of white or natural gray." Later, "Conductors of white or natural gray shall not be used other than as conductors for which identification is required" etc. meaning that a white wire must never be used as the hot wire! (Article 200-2, 200-3, 200-6, NEC 1971.)

The Code also provides that the secondary supply to the home, meaning the service wires from the transformer on the pole, shall be grounded on the supply side of the overcurrent protection device or disconnect, and that the home wiring must not be grounded after it leaves the disconnect. This is a free-hand translation of Art. 250-23.

One of my correspondents, a professor of electrical engineering at a northern university, brought out an interesting point, which could stand a bit of clarification, for which I thank him. This is the somewhat confusing difference between grounded and grounding conductors. unless you watch closely, the Code can be just a little ambiguous along in here!

While both of the "ground" conductors mentioned, the white wire and the green, are grounded, there is a difference in their function. The white wire is a "current-carrying conductor, grounded," and a part of the power circuit. The green

71

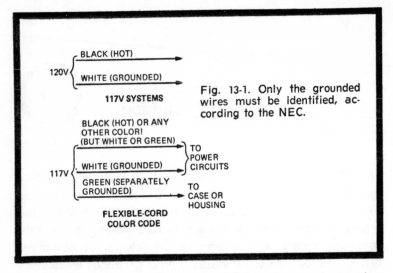

Fig. 13-1. Only the grounded wires must be identified, according to the NEC.

wire, on the other hand, is a "grounded, noncurrent-carrying conductor." It is not a part of the power circuits, and is merely a safety feature!

The Code says "Grounding conductors—shall be arranged so that there is no objectionable passage of current..." It goes on to say that fault currents set up in the grounding conductor under accidental conditions aren't objectionable! (That's nice of 'em.) The aim of this chapter, as it looks to me, is that there should be no normal current flow in the safety ground, but that it must be capable of carrying enough current to trip the circuit-breaker if a fault does occur.

Strangely enough (to electronics types) the Code does not provide for color coding of any wires other than the two ground wires. You can use any colors you want; provisions apply mainly to flexible cords and wires (Art. 400-13, 400-14). The white (or natural gray) is always the one used as the grounded conductor, and the green wire is always the grounding conductor. So, what we get out of this is one fact: outside of the white and green wires, all wires must be considered **hot** (See Fig. 13-1.)

To clear up one more point, the new type 3-prong plug-and-socket combinations, with the round ground pin, should not be used in wiring systems having only two wires—not unless the wires are replaced, which could lead to quite a bit of "wire-pulling" through the walls in the typical home. In most places, you can use flexible conduit or Romex for this, if you use the 3-wire type. It has two insulated conductors, (usually black and white) and a bare wire.

For a strictly Code job, this bare wire, which is the grounding conductor, must be connected to the ground connection of the service wiring, at the service disconnect. It is for cases where new Romex is run to an additional outlet.

There is one exception noted in the Code; Art. 250-50, p. 74: "Exception: for branch-circuit extensions only in existing installations which do not have a grounding conductor, the grounding conductor of a grounding-type receptacle may be grounded to a grounded cold-water pipe near the equipment." This would allow the use of the "3-wire with one round pin" type of receptacles, in systems with only two wires; for laundry rooms, utility rooms, and such places, where a cold-water pipe is nearby for the ground. For this, the green wire in the appliance line cord must be connected to the round pin of the plug; this is the safety ground. The round hole in the new receptacle must be wired to the cold-water pipe. Bare wire can be used here, of the same size as the conductors.

So, there you have the two types of ground. The "power-circuit grounded conductor"—a part of the circuit carrying power, as in Fig. 13-1. As the Code says (Art. 250-25), "The identified conductor is commonly known as 'the white wire'." There is always current flowing in this, when a load is connected and turned on, although it is at ground potential.

The other one is the green wire and should be connected to the same ground point as the white wire, at the service-disconnect unit. This is the point where the service wires enter the building. (Incidentally, this wire will be green only in flexible cords; in the branch wiring it'll probably be a bare wire.) This wire never carries current in normal operation. It carries current only when there is a fault (meaning a short circuit).

It is a good idea to check with your local wiring inspectors as to the ground connection of the safety ground. The Code

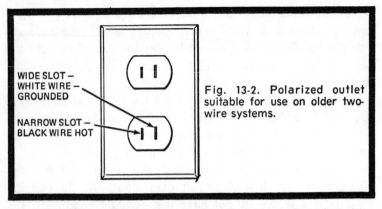

WIDE SLOT —
WHITE WIRE —
GROUNDED

NARROW SLOT —
BLACK WIRE HOT

Fig. 13-2. Polarized outlet suitable for use on older two-wire systems.

recommends connecting this to the same ground as the white wire. In some cases, there may be different interpretations, allowing the use of a different ground for the safety ground. Article 250-23 says, "Grounding connections shall not be made on the load side of the service-disconnecting means." Then they list three "exceptions," one of which we mentioned.

You can install polarized plugs and sockets on the older two-wire systems, with which the majority of the homes in this country are wired. These have one wide blade and one narrow one, so that the plug can be inserted only one way (Fig. 13-2). This is an old system, and has been used for years. The grounded (white) wire must be connected to the wide blade of the pin and the corresponding terminal in the receptacle. On the receptacle itself, the terminal screws will be coded; the ground side will be plated with cadmium or the like so that it looks "white" or slivery. The hot wire will be copper colored. In the new three-pin receptacles, the safety-ground screws will usually have a coating of green paint for identification.

Just remember the differences; a grounded, current-carrying conductor is always the "identified wire" (white). The grounding conductor will be bare in the wiring, and green in the appliance line cord. Any other color of wire should always be considered as hot!

Something Old, Something New-

14

In a lot of homes, wired quite a while ago, they used an invention of the devil called **BX** or flexible metal conduit.

I've used miles of this stuff. Perhaps not miles, but it seemed like it. It's a two- or three-conductor cable (in the home types) covered by a spiral steel sheath. In a correct installation, this sheath is grounded, and also connected to the metal outlet boxes in the walls. The objection, among those who install it, is the difficulty of working it.

You had to cut the sheath with a hacksaw, trying not to cut the wires, leaving enough of them out to make the connections. You also had to put on a clamp that held the sheath tightly to the boxes. (Inspectors had a habit of grabbing the cable and yanking very hard.) Also, it was run not under but through the floor and ceiling joists! This was done with another devilish invention called a "joist drill."

However, there are still a lot of homes wired with this type of cable. Perfectly safe, even though old. If the original wiring was correctly installed, the sheath of the BX cable and all of the metal outlet boxes will be grounded at the service entrance. So, despite a statement to the contrary, you can install the new type "three-hole" receptacles in a wiring system like this. All you have to do is connect the two wires properly (grounded wire to the wide slot, remember). Most of the 3-hole outlets I have seen will automatically make the "third-wire ground" connection when they are screwed down. You can check for this by just looking at the new receptacle. If the green-painted screw is obviously connected to the mounting ears, okay.

The BX wiring should be checked out carefully. A close visual inspection of the service entrance (and all visible BX) should do. You can pull the switch and check the BX sheath for grounding with an ohmmeter. This should be a very low resistance. I don't know whether this is an approved test or not, but you might run a check by disconnecting the grounded wire at the outlet, and then connecting a load, with clip leads from the hot wire to the grounded box. Note the ac line voltage with the load turned on. Now, disconnect it and hook up the regular grounded wire (white). Repeat; if you get the same voltage under load, the ground should be satisfactory. In other words, the sheath-grounding is low-resistance, just like the grounded-wire grounding.

At any rate, with one of the oldest Code wiring systems in the country, you can have all of the safety advantages of the latest thing, the three-wire system, and it will be completely "Code." On general principles, it would be a very good idea to check with your local electrical code. The NFPA book, although considered authoritative, is not in any sense a law. Local rules and regulations do prevail, so make sure.

Some local codes permit using the metal sheath of BX cable for equipment grounds. Others do not because rust and corrosion cause high-resistance connections which get hot enough to start a fire if a live conductor shorts to the sheath.

While we're on the subject, there have been several recent developments in the field of ground fault interrupters (GFIs). For one, the Harvey Hubbell Co. now has a model (GFP-115) that can be plugged into any dual outlet wired for the 3-wire system. The outlet must be rated at least 15A, 117V. This is the "standard-trip" rating of this model, as a circuit-breaker. The trip-rating as a GFI is 5.0 mA. Differential transformers and a solid-state amplifier are used. It is simply plugged into one of the receptacles; a captive screw holds it in place, and automatically makes the safety-ground connection. This goes into the center hole between the outlets.

Any appliance of not more than 15A rating can then be used in safety from the GFI outlet. A test button is provided;

when this is pushed, the pilot light should come on, indicating that the unit is working. Pushing the reset button sets it for use again. Of course, if there is any leakage in whatever you plug into it—drill, saw, extension cord, etc.—the GFI will trip, indicating that the thing isn't safe! If this happens, you'd better find out why, on general principles. Of course, the GFI will protect you from folly, but it might be a long crawl back out from under the house or whatever unpleasant place you have to work!

Somewhere in my filing system, I have a note sent by a friend. It says that the Triplett people have added yet another handy accessory to work with the model 310 miniature VOM. This will go along with the very useful clamp-on ammeter, model 10. The new unit is a leakage tester, for tracing and repairing just such a situation as I've been talking about.

15   Inside The Clothes Dryer

Clothes dryers, like most major appliances, aren't really too complex. They all have the same parts: a large perforated drum turned at a low speed by a motor, a heater and fan to blow hot air through the drum, a thermostat to control the air temperature, and an electrically driven timer to control the entire process.

In the electrically heated dryers, large heating elements are mounted in the air duct, with a fan to force the hot air through the drum. The majority of these use 240V heaters. Elements run from 2000 to 5000 watts. The heating elements have three controls; the switch contacts in the timer, which will probably operate a relay to switch the high currents, and a thermostat acting as a limit switch. This breaks the heater circuit when the temperature rises above the desired point.

So if the problem is that the drum turns but the clothes stay cold, you have one of four possibilities: open switch contacts in one of the three controls just mentioned, or an open heating element. Many of the later-model dryers have multiple-section heaters for different heats. So, the chances of all of these opening at once would be small. A complete loss of heat would most likely be traceable to the three switches.

To check for this, pull the machine out from the wall, pull the line plug, and take the back off. Usually this will be fastened with self-tapping screws around the edges. In a great many units, you'll find a complete wiring diagram pasted to the back or inside the cabinet. With this, it isn't too hard to find the wires going to the heaters and trace them out. With a continuity meter, the various switch contacts can be checked by turning the timer knob manually to the right position.

In the flat-top types with controls mounted on a splash-board (vertical surface at the back of the top) many of the controls will be quite accessible. In several models, the whole top can be slid back and lifted up, exposing all heater wiring, controls, etc. A lot of the wiring, including the timer, will use push-on connectors, which makes it very handy to check.

The thermostat can be hard to get to in some, especially if it is mounted inside the air ducts. However, you can trace the wiring from the timer and controls, and locate the leads to it. Pull these loose and you can check the contacts for continuity. If the dryer is cold, the contacts should be closed, of course. If you get an open-circuit reading across the thermostat leads, its contacts aren't making. Take it off and check the contact surfaces for burning or pitting. If they are badly burnt, it would be best to replace the thermostat.

Filing down the points would change the spacing, and probably make the thermostat lose calibration. Be careful while handling them, since calibration can also be upset by bending the blade. Some units use a snap-action thermostat, making use of what is called the "oil-can" effect; these are not easily upset.

If the drum won't turn, but you can hear the motor running, you've got a belt problem. This is accessible as soon as you take the back off. If the belt has jumped off, check the alignment of the driving and drum pulleys and the motor mounts. Failure or breakage of one of the motor mounts can throw the motor out of line and the belt will jump as soon as it's started the next time.

If the belt is broken, take the old one to an appliance supply house to be sure you get the right length and size replacement belt.

Some units use a spring-loaded idler arm. It moves to tighten the belt and make the drum turn. Check the control linkage, springs, and bearings on this. The whole thing is usually easy to get at, and adjustments are simply mechanical. If the idler arm doesn't hold the belt against the pulleys tightly enough, it will slip, causing rapid wear and short belt life. With the arm engaged, the belt should have only a small amount of slack.

The timers are driven by a small electric motor, similar to the type used in electric clocks, mounted on the back of the switching unit. In many makes, this motor can be replaced without changing the whole timer. Two screws hold them in place, on a bracket.

If the whole timer must be replaced, the push-on connectors make this job a lot easier. Color coding of wires is used extensively, and the whole thing should be shown on the wiring diagram. If this isn't clear enough, or if it doesn't show color coding, make up your own drawing of the wires.

The best way, if a timer must be replaced, is to leave the old one in place until you have the replacement. Then, unbolt the old one and pull it away from the panel, leaving the wires connected. Mount the new unit, and then transfer the wires to it, one at a time. Much less chance of confusion.

Fan or blower problems are usually fairly obvious. If the fan doesn't run, check the belt. Many of these are driven from the drum motor; others have their own small motor. Most of these are mounted on some kind of shock mount—rubber pads, etc.—to prevent excessive noise and vibration. If these mounts have gone bad from old age or heat, the fan blades can hit the sides of the duct, making a terrible roar. It's a good idea to check all rubber mountings like this whenever you have the back off the dryer.

All in all, you shouldn't find any really complex problems in modern clothes dryers. Simple electrical equipment, such as a VOM for checking continuity and ac voltage, will tell you what's going on (or not going on, as the case may be).

Use Your Electrical
Appliances When Abroad

16

Americans travel a lot—pleasure, business, military, and so on. A lot of them like to take their home with them in the form of their electrical appliances—razors, clocks, record and tape players, hair dryers, styling combs, and the like. This can lead to problems in most areas of the world. U.S. electrical things are built to work on 115V 60 Hz power. Not so in a great many other countries.

The rest of the world uses a bewildering variety of power supply voltages and frequencies. Although dc power has been displaced by ac in this country, you may still find it in use in homes of other countries: Spain, Sweden, Austria, Germany, Ireland, and so on. Only in the British Isles is there any semblance of a nationwide standard. They use 230V, 50 Hz ac for residential power.

The undisputed champion for variety would probably be Italy. There, you'll find dc voltages at 110, 125, 150, 160, and 250; and ac supplies of 110, 115, 125, 135, 150, 220 and 260 volts, at either 42, 45, or 50 Hz. France runs them a close second, with 110, 120, 125 and 250 volts dc; and 110, 115, 120, 125, 200 and 230 volts ac at either 25 or 50 Hz. Other countries use similar voltages; all of Europe seems to use 50 Hz, as well as all of Asia and Africa. There are a few "60 Hz enclaves" here and there, such as Taiwan.

This poses problems for our travelers. How and where can they use their electrical appliances? The answer in some cases is "Forget it!" Units that have synchronous motors— clocks, tape recorders, phonographs—will run slow on 50 Hz.

More on this later. One helpful development in the clock and tape recorder line is battery-powered clocks and tape recorders with dc motors.

Other units with "universal-wound" motors can be used on the right voltage. Many of these will even run on dc. Appliances with heating elements, of course, don't care at all about the frequency, as long as the voltage is right.

This brings us to this often asked question: "What can I do to make my appliance work overseas?" Within the limits mentioned, a great many of them can be used very well with a simple addition—something to change the local line voltage to 115-120 volts ac. A simple autotransformer can be used to step down the British 230V line (remember to say "mains" so they'll know what you mean). The power rating of the autotransformer depends on how much the appliance draws. Check the rating plate on yours to see what it needs.

Razors need only very small amounts of power; probably 20-30W. Hair dryers, however, have heating elements as well as fan motors. The motor will draw perhaps 35 watts, but the heating element can take up to 1500 watts. So check it. If the wattage isn't given, just multiply the voltage rating by the amps, and this will be good enough. Recharger units for cordless appliances draw only minute amounts; 2 to 3 watts maximum. So, a very small autotransformer will take care of these very nicely.

I get a lot of inquiries about "making up a simple dropping resistor" for these. It would work, but frankly, I'm not too fond of it. A tapped dropping resistor could be "calibrated" to work with a single appliance, but if one of a different wattage were plugged into it, the voltage would be far off. Such a device would be impractical for high-drain units like hair dryers; your dropping resistor would get hotter than the dryer.

So, the suitably rated autotransformer is probably the most practical solution for low-power units. It wouldn't be too big or too expensive. However, an autotransformer capable of handling a 1500-watt hair dryer would run about 50 pounds in weight! A 100-watt unit weighs only 7 pounds.

FREQUENCY CHANGERS

It is, of course, possible to make frequency changers. All you need is a power supply, an oscillator that will run at the desired frequency and a power amplifier. However, it would be shockingly uneconomical. For high power output, the output transistors alone would probably cost more than the price of a new appliance that would work on the "native" current. This says nothing at all about size, either. A 40-pound, $250 converter running a $19.95 electric razor would not make sense.

To sum up, it would be easiest to select cordless appliances for your overseas journey, if possible. For the rest, check the power ratings on the plate. If they run up around 1000 watts you'll probably be better off leaving them at home. You can get power adapters such as autotransformers in this country. One type is handled by the Franzus Co., Box 395, Shamokin, PA. 12872.

Of course, there are simple solutions. If time is your problem, just lift the phone and say "Bonjour, m'selle. Q'est-ce-que le temps du jour?" Of course, this won't work too well in England; there, the response would probably be "Coo! Wot did 'ee sye?" Of course, you could always listen for Big Ben.

One final cheerful note. By choosing your tour carefully, you can get along very well. The Society Islands in the South Pacific use good ol' 120V 60 Hz power! Aloha.

17 Interlocks and Mental Blocks

The diagnosis of trouble in any automatic appliance looks like a big job, at first. Automatic washers, dryers, and others seem to be pretty complicated. They are, but if you'll take what is often an unusual step—thinking!—it will be a lot easier. There are always certain key reactions that will help give you a handle on the problem.

The basic principle of this is the same in all types of machinery. First, find out what the thing is doing—then, recheck to find out what it isn't doing. A lot of appliances will turn out to be interlocked. That is, if one thing isn't there, this will make something else stop.

All of these units have certain inputs; ac power, hot water, cold water, gas, and so on. These must be present, and in the right quantities, or the thing isn't going to work, or won't work properly. It's built that way intentionally. This feature prevents the machine from going through a normal cycle if one or more of the normal inputs is missing.

In automatic washers, the machine will stop if there isn't enough water in the tube during a certain part of the cycle—rinse, for example. Conversely, it will also stop if there is water in the tub when it shouldn't be there—at the point when the machine should go into spin. The excess water in the tub would put a very heavy drag on the cylinder in the high-speed spin cycle; so, this is interlocked with the water-level indicator.

This can happen if the drain hose or pump is clogged. The pump cannot drain the tub; so the machine will simply stop and sit there waiting for someone to come along and fix it. A similar thing could happen to a dryer. These have two thermostats; one closes when the drum is too cool to bring the dryer up to proper temperature. The other, normally closed, opens if the drum temperature goes too high, to avoid burning up things. If the vent of the dryer becomes clogged, with a bird's nest or something like that, the air can't get out of the machine. With the circulation blocked, the inside temperature will rise, and the upper-cutoff thermostat will turn the whole thing off.

These are all simple things, but very important. I can vouch for that. Not too long ago, a certain wife said to her husband, "My washer won't work." "What's the matter?" said the husband, who had written four books and two correspondence courses on electrical appliances. "How do I know?" replied wife. "It goes through the wash cycle fine, then stops on rinse."

The husband ran the timer switch on the washer through the whole cycle, and noticed that all he got in rinse was a buzz. "Call George and ask him to check it," he called back upstairs to his wife. "After all, it's still in warranty!" and he left for the "office."

When he came home that evening he was met at the door by a wife wearing a very wide grin. "Here" she said, handing him a piece of paper. "George left this note for you!" Printed on it, in large block letters, was "Try turning the water on next time, genius!"

Being blessed with perfect 20-20 hindsight, I (woops—he) immediately knew what had happened. He'd rigged up a plumber's nightmare on the cold-water cock, so that water could be drawn for various things. Since this leaked, as could be expected, he'd formed a habit of turning it off at the sillcock. This, of course, turned off the cold-water supply to the washer at the same time.

Here's what had happened: The machine had gone through wash cycle since this used only hot water. However, the rinse cycle required warm water; both hot and cold valves open at once. Without the cold water, the machine had not filled to the correct level by the time it was ready to go into the rinse cycle. So, with this interlock open, it had simply shut itself off and sat there waiting for further instructions.

To avoid this kind of embarrassing contretemps in the future, watch out for that mental block. Don't take anything for granted. Check for the presence of all of the necessary inputs to the machine; ac, hot and cold water, gas, free vent, clear drain, and so on. These are all simple things, and if you make a methodical checkout on them, you'll fix the "mysterious troubles" that such machinery is prone to.

Always check the simple things first and save the complicated ones for later on when it becomes apparent that they're necessary.

Intermittents—How To Locate Them

18

An intermittent is something which makes intermittent contact in a circuit. It can be a short, but the tougher ones seem to be opens. They can be broken down into two general types—the "physical" or "jar" intermittent, where you can make it act up by tapping the chassis; and the thermal, caused by heat.

The "jar" intermittents are much easier to find. By tapping the chassis very carefully you can find the most sensitive area, and from this point, it's not too hard to locate a guilty part or solder joint. The eraser of a lead-pencil makes a dandy tapper.

Thermals are tougher. Even in a transistor chassis, you're going to find thermal intermittents. This is especially true of those long-term intermittents that cut out once a day. Something in there is getting hot and expanding. The circuit opens (or shorts to other parts) and there you are. In the standard thermal no amount of jarring the chassis (or kicking the cabinet) will faze it.

There are a couple of tricks you can play on these. One is running the set with the ac line voltage just a little above normal. This won't hurt anything unless you leave it on for too long. The high line voltage will raise the dc voltages. It will also raise the temperature of things and make the intermittent more apt to act up. If this doesn't work, try running it with line voltage a little below normal. This leaves things a little cooler than they usually are.

Determine the characteristics of the trouble. Does it cut out once a day, every 2-3 days, every hour or so, etc.?

87

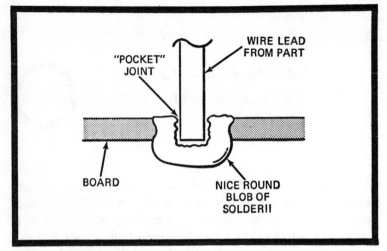

Fig. 18-1. The "pocket" joint is a troublemaker.

Questioning the owner is a very good way to get this information. If this is a long-term intermittent, and irregular, the chances are that it is a thermal.

There's a division here. If the intermittent shows up within a short time after the set's turned on, say 5 to 10 minutes, the chances are that it is in some part which generates its own heat; a current-carrying resistor and so on. Solder joints are frequent offenders in this category.

The other and much more difficult type is the long-term intermittent. These show up at irregular intervals, from hours to days. They're also thermal, but are caused by conducted heat—from other parts on the chassis getting hot. This heat is conducted through the chassis or the air. In "touchy" intermittents, the frequency of cutout often depends greatly on the ambient temperature.

In both types, heat is the troublemaker. It causes physical movement of the part, making or breaking contact. This can be as little as a thousandth of an inch, if it's inside a resistor, coil, or capacitor, but it's enough! Printed-circuit-board solder joints are frequent offenders. A pocket joint (see Fig. 18-1) can make perfect contact. But if the board expands slightly, whammo. If you suspect this, you can get out the "shotgun";

remelt and resolder all solder joints in the area of the trouble. You may never know which one it was, but you'll fix it.

ISOLATION

The first thing you must do is isolate the area of trouble. From the characteristics, you know about where it is. Observing the characteristics will give you clues. Now, check every part of the circuit that could affect that particular function.

Now, see if you can make it show up. To do this, you can either apply more heat or less heat. The reaction to these tests will give you a lot of data, and that's what you need. You can apply heat with a heat lamp, by touching the suspected part with the tip of a soldering iron, or by blowing hot air on it with a heat gun or old hair dryer. Cooling is much easier. The spray-can coolant is a very useful weapon for locating intermittents.

Here's a good example. I had a Zenith color TV set on the bench. The picture flickered on and off at highly irregular intervals, leaving a white screen. This was a very fast flicker, sometimes repeated three or four times. After doing this, it would play for a couple of hours. In fact, it sat on the bench under observation for two days; no flicker! Fortunately for my production ratio, I was working on other things at the same time!

Then I got after it in earnest. Turning it on, I waited. This time, it started to flicker in only about 20 minutes. A quick check with the scope and a crystal-detector probe showed a steady signal at the i-f input and a severe flicker at the video detector output. So, I had it pinned down; it was in the i-f.

Now I made thermal tests. With a junk hair dryer which still worked, I blew hot air on the i-f stages. On the first and second stages, no result. As soon as I hit the last i-f stage and detector, wham! It started flickering like mad. To verify this, I blew spray coolant on it. The picture came back as steady as a rock. Now I had it!

The i-f stage in these sets can be taken out in toto by pulling off some push-on connectors and taking out three screws. Making up a set of connecting leads, I put it on the bench and turned it on. Despite a tendency to oscillate, it worked well enough for testing. I checked each part in the output stage, by touching it with the tip of a soldering iron. When I hit the output transistor, out it went!

Verifying this, I sprayed the thing with coolant. It came back on. Replacing this transistor cleared up the trouble. Hooking the original transistor to a curve tracer, it checked perfectly. Heating it with the soldering iron, in about 20 seconds it went to the horizontal line; it was opening up internally! Spraying it with the coolant brought it back again. I could repeat this as often as I wanted to. For a definite check, I warmed up my replacement transistor with the soldering iron. Absolutely no change in the picture.

About this time, someone will say "But you'll ruin those delicate transistors, heating them up like that with a soldering iron." To which I can reply, "Possibly so. However, I have never damaged one yet with this method, and I've tried!"

I will admit that I've been guilty of saying that there was no such thing as an intermittent transistor. I stopped this; people kept sending me intermittent transistors, and I kept finding them in sets I was working on.

They can be thermal. In fact, a post-mortem analysis of the case of the Zenith brought out an interesting fact. The reason it sat on the bench and played for two days was that during those days the shop air conditioner was running, and blowing right at it! On the day that it started cutting out, the air conditioner was turned off! This comparatively small difference in the ambient temperature was enough to make it start acting up.

There are many ways you can go after this kind of trouble; don't neglect any of them. You can jar it, you can change the supply voltage, or you can heat it or cool it. Somewhere in this list, you should be able to find something that will make it show up. When you do, you've practically got it licked.

90

All About Timers

19

The control center of any automatic electrical appliance that offers multiple functions is the timer. Each "thing" must be turned on and off at the proper point in the cycle. In an automatic washer, for instance, this would include water valves, the motor, drain pump, clutches for changing speed from wash to spin, and even the timer driving motor itself. When it reaches the end of the cycle, it turns itself off.

If you have troubles in any machine like this, the first thing to do is to isolate the function that isn't working. For example, the hot-water valve. A symptom here would be cold water in the tub after the timer has gone through the wash position. If the machine has a **temperature** selector switch (**hot** and **warm**), this would be set to **warm** for the cold-water-in-the-tub symptom. If the selector switch was set to hot, the symptom would probably be "no water at all" since only the **hot** valve opens then. (First, check to make sure that the hot water faucet is turned on.)

Check the wiring diagram on the back of the machine, and locate the hot-water solenoid. (Follow the hoses.) There are several ways of checking this. Pull the ac plug, and pull one wire from the solenoid. Most of these have push-on connectors. Check the coil for continuity with an ohmmeter. If this is good, follow the wiring up to the timer. It may go through the **hot-warm** selector switch; some of these control only the cold-water solenoid, however.

Most machines have very plainly color coded wiring. Follow the hot-water valve lead to the contacts on the timer. Be sure that all of the push-on connectors are firmly seated.

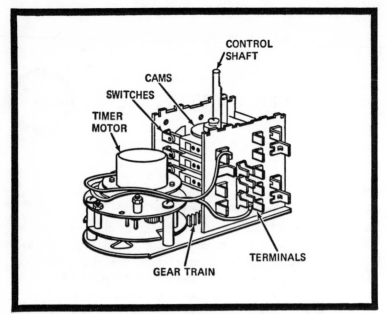

Fig. 19-1. Typical timer assembly, with motor and contacts.

Wiring troubles are comparatively rare, but check for them just the same.

Next, you can turn the timer knob to the beginning of the wash portion of the cycle. The hot-water valve should be open, filling the tub. Check across the timer contacts with the ohmmeter.

A better test for contacts is to clip the ac voltmeter across them (insulated clips please!), and then plug the machine in. With the contacts open, you will normally read the full line voltage across them (unless another switch somewhere in the circuit is open). However, when the contacts should be closed, there should be absolutely no voltage drop across them. If you see a low ac voltage reading, this indicates that the contacts are dirty. You're reading the drop across the resistance of the dirt.

This means trouble. The resistance of the poor contact generates heat, the heat burns the contacts even more, and you're in a vicious circle. In a great many of these timers, the contacts are easy to get at. Figure 19-1 shows a typical timer assembly. You can clean up the contacts with a point file, fine sandpaper, or even an emery board. Smooth them off to a high polish for best contact.

Turn the timer knob by hand to open and close the contacts. Check to make sure that the contacts meet absolutely flat, or parallel, for maximum contact area. If necessary, bend the contact arms very slightly so that they do meet properly. Contact closure should be firm, so that the arm bends just a tiny bit, to jam the contacts tightly together. Figure 19-2 shows how this type of cam and lever actuator works. As you can see here, some of them use single-pole switches. Be sure that both sides are in good shape.

The timer drive motor is a small sealed synchronous unit, a lot like those used in electric clocks. A gear train is used to give the little motor enough torque to drive the cam assembly. We find very little trouble with these motors, although if the machine has been visited by lightning, the winding may be

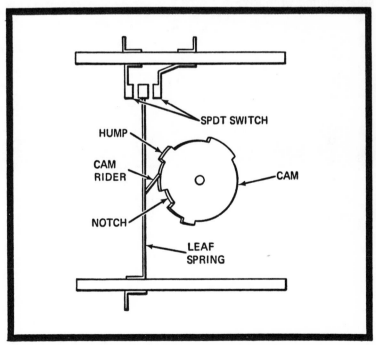

Fig. 19-2. Cam drives contact arms in timer, as shown here.

open. Normally, neither the motor or gear train will require lubrication.

This type of motor isn't repairable; the whole motor must be replaced. In most units, this can be done without even taking the timer off. Take out two or three screws and it drops off into your hand. Exact duplicate replacements must be used, of course. These are available from the distributor for this make of appliance, or from independent part wholesalers.

As I said, we have very few troubles with motors like this. When we do, though, it's sometimes a dandy. In one notable case, an air-conditioning system had a very puzzling intermittent. Most of the time it worked perfectly. Once in a while, it would start, then shut down. After much head scratching and some not-too-nice language, we "caught it in the act." These tiny motors are synchronous and they always start in the same direction. This one had to start a timer and run through a couple of operations so that the system could start cooling properly.

Clean Up The Cleaners

20

The home vacuum cleaner is a simple thing. Let it get out of order, though, and you've got troubles. So, let's see how to check one for proper operation.

All vacuum cleaners are alike. They have a fan, an electric motor to turn it, and a system of hose, ducts, a dust bag, and a case to hold the thing together. That's all. To work as they should, they must have a free flow of air through all of these parts. Let it clog up, and you lose suction.

For a quick-check, turn it on and put the palm of your hand over the end of the hose. It should pull your hand against the hose with a solid "thunk"! The motor will normally slow down just a little. The sound of the motor is a dandy clue; it should have a healthy howl. If it grunts and groans, and sounds as if it were pulling a heavy load, something is at least partially blocking one of the air passages.

You've got several possibilities: the hose and staff (the long metal tube), the bag, and the housing itself. Eliminate the hose first; with the motor running, pull it out of the housing. If the motor suddenly speeds up and sounds free, the hose is clogged. You can plug it into the blow outlet on the other side of the housing. Don't do this in the house! If the dirt comes loose, you'll blow it all over the place. Do it outside or in the garage.

If the hose is okay, check the bag. These are cloth or paper, but they must be porous so that the air can get out, while trapping the dust. If they have been used too long, the tiny pores may be stopped up. Try a new bag. If it's cloth, turn it inside out, dump the dust, and then beat it as clean as possible.

If this doesn't get it, open the cleaner housing and check the filters; there will be at least one. These are small porous discs made of paper, cloth, or fine wire mesh that are placed over the motor to stop fine dust that may get through the bag. If they're loaded with dust, either clean them or put in a new one. You may find another one at the outlet opening of the housing. Same here; be sure that air can get through it.

In practically all modern cleaners, the air flow goes through the motor itself. This is done to help cool it. The incoming air goes through the bag and the filter first, of course. In time, enough fine dust can get through and stick to the motor to partially clog the air flow.

This can get worse, of course. In the inside-bag or tank cleaners, if the bag comes off the mounting clamp, all of the dirt will promptly go to the motor. This makes quite a mess, and stops the flow of air almost completely.

The cure is a thorough cleanup. The easiest way is to take the thing to the nearest filling station and blow the dirt out with a high-pressure air hose. Of course, if you have another cleaner, or a Shop-Vac, you can use it to clean this one up. A dry paintbrush is a good tool to get the dust out. If some of it has solidified, it can be very carefully dug out with a stick or small screwdriver. Be very careful not to gouge the motor windings, leads, etc., since these are exposed.

Most of the tank or canister-type cleaners have the motor mounted on a sheet-metal plate in the housing. If the motor isn't accessible when you open the case to change bags, you can get it out by taking out three or four small screws around the edge of the mounting plate. These are usually visible. If they're not, and the cleaner has a thick soft rubber gasket around the lip, lift the edge of this gasket and look under it; the mounting screws may be hidden under there.

The older models need oiling at infrequent intervals. Most of the newer ones have permanently sealed bearings. Check the instruction book to make sure. Of course, if you can see a tiny hole in each end-bell of the motor, that should tell you! About two drops of oil every six months is plenty. Don't overoil; excess oil around the motor and fan will pick up dust and cake it everywhere.

Many units have enclosed fans; the air will come through the motor, then into the center of the impeller fan, and out of a duct on the rim. If you hear a clattering noise as the motor runs, take the cover off the fan, and see if the impeller is hitting the case, or what else may be wrong. Once in a while, dust will cake on the blades, and some of it may be thrown off, hitting the cover. If there is any accumulation on the blades, scrape it off. The dirt throws the fan off balance.

As with everything else, I have a favorite prop story about vacuum cleaners: Many years ago, I worked in St. Louis for an appliance dealer. I got a call to go see a little old German lady. When I got there, I found that she spoke practically no English. However, like all of us there at that time, I had a smattering of PlattDeutsch so we got along.

"Was ist los, Frau Schmitt?" I asked. "Meine Staubsanger is ausgeschpielten!" she said, indicating that her vacuum cleaner was kaput. "Das is alles recht" I said. "Ich willst begebenst es." She went to the closet and wheeled out a "stick" type vacuum cleaner, a Hoover, I think—one of the kind with a handle and a large cloth bag. The bag looked suspiciously fat. I felt it—just like a sandbag!

With some difficulty, I lugged it out into the yard, and got it off. There must have been 40 pounds of dust in it! I emptied it into the ashpit and went back. I hooked it up, and it howled happily. I cleaned up the dirt I'd spilled on the floor, and she beamed at me. "Ach, das is wunderbar!"

I showed her how to take the bag off and empty it. She looked puzzled. I said "Was ist? Die verkaufer sollte gezeigt du?" (What is this? Didn't the salesman show you how to do this?) "Nein, nein!" I went off happily munching on a big handful of Springerle (it was near Christmas).

The moral of this, of course, is **read the instruction book.**

21 Electric Heaters And Safety Devices

Even in homes with central heating, there are a lot of small portable electric heaters around. These are used for special purposes. For example, daughter likes the bathroom very warm, but the rest of the family doesn't want to swelter. These are very common in England; they call them "Electric Fires." Incidentally, these are the only electrical appliances which are almost 100 percent efficient. There is practically no loss at all. What we want is heat. So we connect a resistance element across the line, and it gets hot. Nothing is wasted.

Heating elements come in a large assortment of sizes and shapes—coiled wire, ribbon, sealed types, and so on. They're all exactly the same, except for the wattage. Just resistance wire, usually an alloy called nichrome—nickel and chromium. The wattage of a heating element depends on its resistance. The lower the resistance, the higher the current and the more heat.

As far as diagnosis of electrical faults is concerned, they're really pretty elementary. They're either good or open. (Or since they're electrical, they can be intermittent!) There are only a few things to go bad; line cord, switch, or heating element. Easy to check out with an ohmmeter or a simple neon trouble lamp.

Most of the troubles will be in the things like broken line cords, open heating elements, or dirty switches. Due to the high currents, a dirty switch contact or loose connection will cause trouble. They will arc, and this can cause heavy interference in nearby TV and radio sets. If they are allowed to arc for too long a time, the contact will burn open.

Loose connections to the ends of the heating elements cause a lot of problems. These are usually made with a long bolt. It goes through a hole in the metal frame, with ceramic insulators. On the top side, the end of the heating element is fastened between two flat washers, held by a nut. Below the insulators, the line cord is fastened in the same way, between two flat washers, held by two nuts. If either of these works loose, or wasn't properly tightened to start with, the connection will arc. This can actually weld the nuts to the threads so that you can't move them, either to take them off or tighten them.

I ran into one of these not too long ago. I could get the line-cord connector off, but the other end had been arcing too long. The nut was firmly welded to the threads and the element was very loose. (The idea is to get the end of the element loose without breaking it.) In the end, I managed to unwind a couple of turns of the flat ribbon element, and get enough of it out of the cabinet to clamp the bolt in a vise. Then, I sawed the head of the bolt off. The space was so small that I had to use a special razorblade saw, with a very thin blade.

The better grade of heaters have safety devices. Many have thermostats which can be adjusted for any amount of heat desired. Others have special switches, for high, medium or low heats; these switch the heating elements into various combinations. For example, one that I know of has two 1 kW elements. For low heat, one element is turned on. For medium heat, both are connected in series across the 120V line. For high heat, both are connected in parallel.

Safety devices are also used. If one of these heaters was sitting on a carpeted or plastic covered floor, and tipped over face down, it could set the floor on fire. So, a device called a "tip switch" is used. Most of these are pretty simple. On one make, it's just a little rod sticking through the bottom of the case. The top of the rod holds a spring switch closed, as long as the case is upright. If it falls over, the spring-loaded rod moves down and the switch opens.

This can cause problems while you're working on one if you don't know they use a tip switch. You may replace an element, and then try to get it to heat up while lying on its back on the bench. If it won't work, check to see if it has a tip switch.

Replacement heating elements can be purchased at any electrical supply or hardware store. Be sure to check the wattage rating of the original, and get one exactly like it. This rating should be on the rating plate on the back of the case, near the point where the line cord goes in. If necessary, you can use a different type of element; a flat ribbon in place of a coiled wire, or vice versa. Just be sure that you mount the element tightly on the ceramic insulators.

When replacing line cords, check the wattage rating. You must use a cord which has wire big enough to carry the current without getting hot itself. For the smaller types, No. 14 wire is good, but for the bigger ones you'd better use either No. 12 or No. 10 stranded wire. Older ones use asbestos-insulated wire with a heavy braided jacket. Newer models use a plastic insulated cord, like the zipcord on TV line-cords, but much bigger.

Reversing AC Motors

Electric motors designed for dc will often run the other way if the battery polarity is reversed. How do you reverse the rotation of an ac motor? In any one of several ways. Some ac motors aren't easily reversible: synchronous types as used in clocks, phonograph turntables, and so on. Some of these can be reversed, if necessary, by taking them apart and putting the field and frame back upside down. You can make a phono turntable run backward by doing this; especially if the motor has been taken apart for cleaning.

In the common repulsion-induction fractional-horsepower motor, used on many larger appliances, the rotation can be reversed by reversing the leads of the starter winding only. A lot of replacement-type motors have the starter leads brought out to a terminal box on the frame, just for this purpose. Only the starter-winding leads need be switched; the running windings don't care which way the thing goes. In fact, with the starter winding disconnected and power applied, the motor can be started either way by spinning the shaft by hand. In service work, motor reversing isn't too common, but it's handy to know how, if you have to.

There are quite a few applications which need an easily reversible motor. Garage door openers and TV antenna rotators are two examples. The motors used for this purpose are basically all the same, though sizes differ with the power needed. This is called a "capacitor-run" motor and has two windings. Figure 22-1 shows the circuit. Both of the windings stay in-circuit at all times; one isn't disconnected by the starter switch.

The running capacitor causes a phase shift of the voltage and current across it. This type of motor actually operates as a

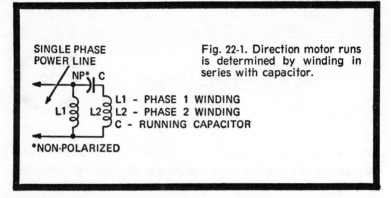

SINGLE PHASE
POWER LINE

NP* C

L1 - PHASE 1 WINDING
L2 - PHASE 2 WINDING
C - RUNNING CAPACITOR

L1 L2

*NON-POLARIZED

Fig. 22-1. Direction motor runs is determined by winding in series with capacitor.

two-phase motor, though the ac line supply is single-phase. This type of operation gives the motor far greater efficiency, by improving the power factor. For a given amount of power, this motor draws much less current from the line.

These motors can be reversed by simply switching the connections of the two windings to the hot side of the line; the common stays connected to the other side. In TV antenna rotators, this is done by a simple manual switch. Figure 22-2 shows how. (These are low-voltage motors that run on 24V ac

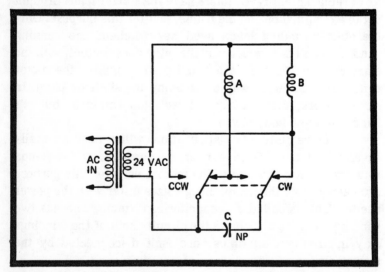

Fig. 22-2. Motor reversing scheme for antenna rotator. Capacitor does the job.

from a transformer.) With the switch in the CW position, winding A is connected directly to the line, and winding B is connected through capacitor C. With the switch turned to CCW position, A is now fed through the capacitor, and B directly from the line. In the typical antenna rotator, C is a non-polarized electrolytic capacitor of about 100 uF, rated at 150V ac. Motors are small and run the thing through gear trains.

For heavier loads, such as garage-door openers, the motors will be bigger; still geared down for more power. They run directly from the ac line. However, circuitry and operating principles are exactly the same. If one winding is connected directly to the hot side of the line and the other through the capacitor, the motor runs one way. Reverse these connections and it runs the other way. Switching can be done by a relay, actuated by a radio-control receiver.

Some of the early models of these units used limit switches. Once started, the motor had to run all the way through the cycle, hitting the limit switch and tripping it before the motor could be reversed. In later versions, limit switches are still used—to be sure the machinery stops when the door reaches the end of its travel, either up or down. However, directional control is now possible; the door can be stopped and started in the other direction.

When the command pulse is received from the transmitter, the receiver starts the motor running. If the door was down, it goes up, and vice versa. However, now the direction of travel can be reversed by pushing the transmitter button again. The door will stop and start in the other direction. (Which is handy, if it happens to be coming down on your foot or the car top.)

Many late models use solid-state switching. Figure 22-3 shows a diagram of a circuit using two triacs, one for up and another for down. Motor windings are arranged just as before; the only difference lies in the addition of the current-limiting resistor (R_s) in series with motor capacitor C_m.

In this circuit, if the "up" triac is switched on, winding A gets current through the capacitor, and winding B directly

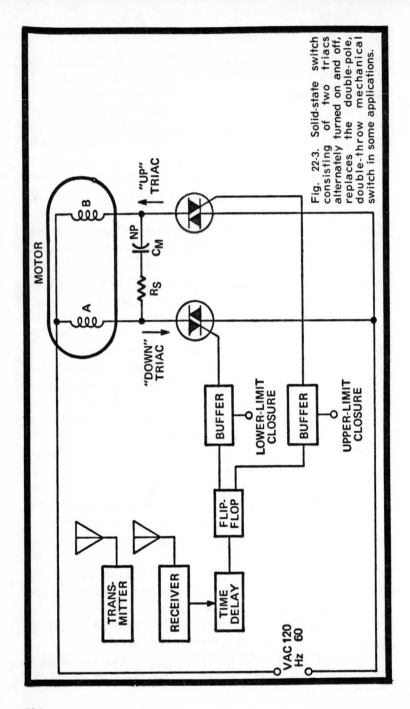

Fig. 22-3. Solid-state switch consisting of two triacs alternately turned on and off, replaces the double-pole, double-throw mechanical switch in some applications.

from the triac. For "down," the action is the same with winding B drawing current through the capacitor. The switching between up and down is done by the flip-flop circuit in the receiver. Similar methods are used in smaller appliances which need reversing motors; drills and so on.

The triac reversing circuit shown here comes from the RCA Solid State Power Circuits Designers Handbook, Technical Series SP-52.

Floor Polishers
And Carpet Scrubbers

A lot of homes now have a combination of floor coverings; partly hardwood and partly carpeting. Cleaning carpets was once done by large gentlemen pushing monstrous machines back and forth over them. There were rental machines, but even these were pretty hefty, up to around 75 pounds. Now, we have home versions, which will not only scrub carpets, but polish and wax wood floors. With the new tough, lightweight plastics, they're light enough to handle with ease.

These are pretty simple machines. They look like an upright vacuum cleaner. A plastic tank on the handle holds the cleaning fluid; a valve on the handle lets the operator use any amount needed. A small motor drives a large round brush or a pair of brushes. These are built into a compartment so that the cleaning fluid can be dribbled down over them and to the floor without spraying the vicinity.

In operation, the machine actually "rides" on the brushes; a pair of small wheels are generally mounted on the back of the case for easy transport. Either carpet cleaning compound or a special thin floor wax can be used in the tank. Heavy waxes will clog the valves and make a cleanup necessary.

For applying wax and polishing wooden floors, large felt pads are attached to the bottom of the brushes. Most people use two sets, one for applying wax and a dry set for the polishing.

You'll find some unusual things in the motors and brush drives. In the single-brush machine, a large eccentric counterweight is used, to balance the brush and keep the machine from vibrating too much. In this model, the brush itself has an eccentric drive so that the brush revolves and actually moves back and forth at the same time. This leaves a track of small circles on the floor.

In the two-brush machines, the brushes are usually built so they rotate in opposite directions. This keeps the machine from wanting to "skate" to one side when it's running. This also leads to some novel designs and features. In one popular model, the motor has a shaft coming out of each end, with a worm gear on it. These go into small gearboxes, where they drive pinions which turn the brushes. Other models use straight gearboxes, and take advantage of the fact that in a multiple gear train, every other gear turns in the same direction, and the ones between opposite.

In the first machine, the brushes are screwed onto the ends of the shaft. A shaft turning counterclockwise must have right-hand threads, and one turning clockwise must have left-hand threads. Otherwise, the brushes will unscrew themselves while the machine is running. If you take the brushes off one of these, be sure that you have the one with the correct threads, or it won't start on the shaft. If it won't go, try it on the other shaft. Other types have brushes which bolt to flanges on the ends of the driving shafts, or slip over splines and are held in place by spring clips, etc. If you can't see any bolts or clips on the hubs of the brushes, they are very likely to be the screw-on type.

"Hydraulically," these are pretty simple. The cleaning fluid is poured into the tank, which can be taken off the handle by opening the latches. The bottom of the tank fits into a receptacle, and the fluid comes out through a small pipe, also fitting into a hole in the bottom of the receptacle. There is a control valve, actuated by a long rod going to the top of the handle. Sometimes, this is on the handle, or in the bottom of the tank itself. It's usually a simple flapper valve.

The only problems you'll find in this part is leakage in the valve, which is mostly due to something getting into the tank and lodging on the valve seat. This can be cleaned out by draining the tank and turning it upside down. The obstruction can be pushed out with a thin rod.

The pipes leading to the brush compartment can be clogged by anything that gets in. These can be cleaned out by running a wire through them.

Electrical troubles are standard. The most common one is probably breakage of the line cord, from continued pulling and flexing. Since these machines are used on damp floors, make a careful inspection of the line cord at regular intervals. If you see any cracks or breaks in the jacketing or insulation, replace the whole cord. Don't take chances.

The on-off switch is usually a slide or toggle type, mounted on the top of the handle. They do wear out from continual use. Replace with identical types, since they usually fit into slots in the handle. Most of them are mounted on a small plate, held to the handle by screws.

If the machine has a gearbox, it will be filled with a fairly heavy cream lubricant. If you find traces of grease on the floor or on the brushes, take it apart. You'll probably find that some of the screws holding the cover plates on the gearboxes have loosened from the vibration, and dropped out, allowing the grease to leak. In some cases, you'll have to take the cover plate off, clean the edges, and replace the gaskets. If you happen to have a tube of soft Permatex in your garage, it will often make very good gaskets for these little boxes.

Hardware
Noise—A Type of TVI

Outside of certain commercials, one of the things that annoys TV viewers the most is interference or noise in the picture. It comes in all shapes and sizes; from older cars, home electrical appliances, and so on. Anything in the house can be tracked down, and identified, by simply turning it on and off. Filtering can then be used to clear it up. Some interference can come from outside sources, though. We used to call this "hash," but now I suppose we should say noise pollution owing to other connotations from the four-letter version.

An irate reader wrote: "I've got so much interference on my TV set that I don't like to watch it. There are two wide bands of dots and streaks that roll slowly up the picture. They interfere with the sound, and even make the picture roll at times. Looks like ignition noise, but I don't think it is. What can I do about it?"

Complain loudly to the power company. I've seen this a great many times. The polite name for it is hardware noise. It's caused by old or defective equipment on the ac lines feeding your house. You'll notice that the interference shows two bands of dots, meaning that it has a characteristic 120 Hz frequency. Without going into too much detail, it's due to a corona discharge. Not on your home's service wiring, which is 230V maximum in most places, but on the feeders or tertiary lines which supply the pole stepdown transformers. These lines are typically 7.6 kV.

Several things can cause it, including defective or cracked insulators; but probably the most frequent offender is the terminals on the transformers themselves. If these are old, or not correctly designed, the corona discharge takes place inside the transformer, above the oil, from the shank of the bolt to the metal case. I have seen some "horrible examples" of these after they'd been replaced, and the shank of the terminal bolt is actually pitted and eaten away by the corona! There are newer types, designed to prevent this; they have plastic insulation, etc. on the shank of the bolt. Your power company probably even has a training film on this, which shows all of the effects and how to cure them.

The reason for the 120 Hz effect is simple. The corona discharge takes place twice during each cycle of the voltage; once on the positive peak and again on the negative peak. Each peak generates the corona discharge, which in turn generates a burst of high-amplitude rf signals, which cover all frequencies. We're going to do something with this effect in a moment.

The first step should be to file a complaint, in writing, with your local power company. Tell them you have hardware noise, and they'll know what you're talking about. Most companies have noise locating equipment, and it shouldn't take them long to find the offending unit.

If you want to try finding it yourself, there are a couple of ways. Drive around the area with a radio-equipped car, or even a portable radio. Set the dial off-station, somewhere near 800 kHz. For some reason, this noise peaks at that frequency. When you find a place where the noise is very loud, turn the dial of the set back and forth. It will usually be of such a high amplitude that you won't be able to use "loudness" alone to pin it down.

When you get closer to the source, the noise will start to spread; it will cover more and more of the dial. For example, if you get noise from 600 to 900 kHz, you're getting closer, but you're not there yet. Keep on looking and tuning, and when you find a place where you can get nothing but noise from one end of the dial to the other, you're getting warm—really warm.

Find the nearest pole. If it has a transformer on it, so much the better. Listen to the noise, and hit the pole a sound whack with a heavy hammer. If this changes the noise, there you are.

Second method. If you have a highly directional TV antenna with a rotator, turn it all the way around, and watch the screen. Find the direction where the noise is most intense. Make a line along this bearing, on a city map. Now locate a friend with an antenna of the same type. Take a bearing on the noise with his antenna. Draw this on the map. At the point where the lines cross, there's the noise. If you can get a third bearing, preferably at a point distant from the first two, you can pin it down even more closely. We used this method on a very bad case, some time ago, and pinned it down to a very bad insulator on a pole almost two miles away. Some nut had shot the insulator with a high-powered rifle!

Due to the fact that power lines make excellent long-wire antennas, you may run into some ambiguity in your bearings. In fact, it's more likely that you'll see a triangle instead of a single point where they cross. At any rate, you're in the ballpark.

Go to the general area where the noise is originating and then switch to the car radio or portable. Use the frequency spread of the noise as the indicator and follow the power line until you find the pole where the noise covers the whole dial. There you are. Look for a little metal tab or label on the pole. This will give you the number, and you can report it to the power company.

25   Electric Carving Knives

The electric carving knife is a handy thing. It can even make Pop look good when he carves the Thanksgiving turkey or slices fresh bread smoothly. They're pretty simple things; a little motor, a wee gearbox to change round-and-round to back-and-forth (rotary to reciprocal), a pair of blades, and a plastic box to hold the whole thing together. There are two types, ac-powered and battery operated, usually called electric and cordless, although both are, obviously, electric.

Repairing one that won't work is pretty simple. The first thing to do is take out the blades. If you don't and if it wasn't running, but starts up suddenly, you may get to be known as Three-Finger from now on.

The cases are usually easy to open. They're made in two parts; one holds the motor, gearbox, etc., and the other is just a cover. Look for small, recessed screws at each end, usually Phillips.

Remove all visible screws, and then (gently!) try to pry the cover off. If it won't come off, don't use muscle. There's another screw or fastener that you haven't found yet. Some cases have a small tongue on one end of the cover, which slips into a slot on the other half. If one end comes loose, try pulling on it gently, and it will come out. In certain makes, you'll find screws hidden under nameplates, labels, and so on. Keep on looking; they're there somewhere.

In a dead one, first find out if you're getting power to the motor. Check for ac voltage where the line cord goes into the case, or read the battery voltage. If it checks out, test the switch. Most switches are spring-return or pushbutton types so the thing won't keep on running if you drop it. A lot of these are built so that you can take them apart by removing a couple of little screws. The contacts are then visible, for cleaning and adjustment.

Most of the ac models, and some of the cordless types, have small brush-type motors. Check the brushes and commutator. Brushes must be long enough and make firm contact with the commutator. Many have flexible leads; check them to make sure they aren't open or shorting to something. Brush holders are usually the open type, so you can see any troubles. The brushes are often held down by small springs.

If the commutator is badly pitted or dirty, clean it up with fine sandpaper after you get the motor running. If it's smooth and shiny, don't mess with it; it's all right. These motors seldom need lubrication. If the rotor is stiff, or labors, check the gearbox first. If it must be oiled, one drop on each end is plenty.

Some cordless models use little sealed dc motors. If you can get the full battery voltage across the motor leads but the motor will not run at all, disconnect one motor lead and check for continuity. If the motor is open, replace it. In fact, if you do get continuity, but it won't run with normal input voltage, replace it. You can't take them apart. (They're like an egg; you can take 'em apart, but getting them back together is something else.)

All of the cordless models use rechargeable batteries, usually nickel-cadmium types. These are permanently connected together with welded straps. The 5-cell 7-volt unit seems to be the most common. If the dc voltage is low, measured at the motor with the switch on (full load), check each cell of the battery, holding the switch on. If you read the normal 1.4 volts across four of them, and the meter shows a reverse polarity across one cell, or zero voltage, that cell is dead, and the whole unit must be replaced. All should read practically the same voltage, within about 5 percent or less.

If all cells show low voltage, the battery could be discharged. Recharge it overnight, then recheck. It would be a good idea to check the charging unit first of all. Plug it in and

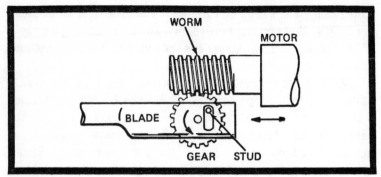

Fig. 25-1. Worm gear converts rotary motion to reciprocating. One blade shown; other on other side of gear.

read the dc voltage across its terminals, no-load. This should be just a little more than the battery voltage. Say about 8 volts for a 7-volt battery and so on. To check the charger for current, connect a small pilot light across the terminals; for a 7V unit use a No. 47 (6-8V, 150 mA). If the bulb lights to a fairly good brightness, the charger can supply normal current. Most of these are trickle chargers, at about 150 to 200 mA maximum.

If the charger is dead, check its line cord; it could be broken at the point where it goes into the housing. Some of these go inside the housing and connect to the rectifier unit with flexible leads. If the ac voltage is present, but no dc output, replace the charging unit. This is literally a black box, sealed so you can't get into it.

The gearboxes are about as simple as you can get. Most of them have only a worm cut into the end of the motor shaft, which drives a gear, usually made of plastic so that it will take the wear. This gear has two small studs, one on each side. These slip into slots in the ends of the knife blades, as shown in Fig. 25-1. This causes the reciprocating motion of the blades. Replacement gears are available, and easy to install. If one blade moves but the other doesn't, one of the studs is broken off.

The gearbox is usually just a cavity molded in half the case. A thin metal cover holds the grease inside. If you find grease leaks, check for missing screws in the cover or a broken gasket. In emergencies, you can cut new gaskets out of paper or plastic.

The blade mountings and slides are usually made out of nylon or Teflon, or something like that. They are not lubricated. Make sure that they can slide freely. The blades are specially grounded, and are normally "self-sharpening" as they rub against each other. If they need sharpening, take them apart, and find the flat side. Use a very smooth oil stone, fine-grained, and hold the blade perfectly flat on the stone. Only a few strokes back and forth on the stone will bring back the cutting edge. Most of them are serrated for easier cutting. Do not try to sharpen from the serrated side.

26   Electronic Matches

Electronic principles are popping up all over these days. Now, they're in your pocket and everywhere else. Here are two applications.

The first is a fully electronic lighter. It's fueled by butane, which isn't new. But in place of the old "thumb-buster" spark wheel, this one has a fully electronic ignition system—actually

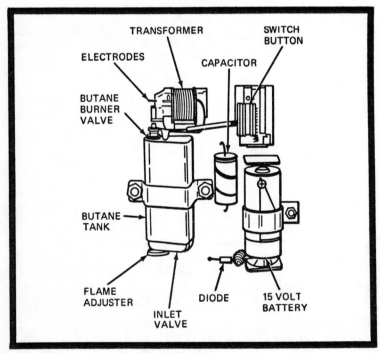

Fig. 26-1. Electronic lighter.

a super-miniaturized version of the capacitor-discharge ignition system used on racing cars! Figure 26-1 shows an exploded view—one battery, one capacitor, a diode, and a stepup transformer, with spark electrodes to do the actual igniting.

All this is operated by the switch button, which opens the butane burner valve at the same time that it fires the spark. The whole thing is compact, no larger than other lighters.

The second device is a lighter with even fewer parts, and is used to ignite gas flames for welding torches, stoves, or any kind of gas-burning device. It works on another well known principle of electronics; this time the heart of the device is a special piezoelectric element. When a piezoelectric crystal is compressed, or struck, it generates a pulse of voltage. In the application we're most familiar with, this reaction makes music in a phono cartridge.

Figure 26-2 is a cross section of the heart of one of these units. This is a hand-held type, for any application requiring portability. A specially designed piezoelectric element, in the form of a rod, is mounted so that two crystals have their positive ends connected together. This places two elements effectively in parallel, to increase the current flow.

A hammer is mounted, with a spring, so that it can be cocked and then tripped to strike the end of the piezoelectric

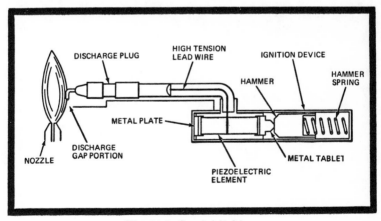

Fig. 26-2. Crystal lighter.

unit. When it does, a high voltage is generated. This is fed through a series resistor to the arc electrodes at the tip, the "discharge plug." The resistor is included to make the arc more efficient in igniting a gas-air mixture. It prolongs the arc discharge.

There's not much of anything to service on these! About the only thing that can make trouble is an accumulation of dirt or grease between the arc electrodes. These can be cleaned by carefully poking a toothpick between them. This unit actually develops up to 14 kilovolts!

The unit shown here is a home device, intended for lighting gas stoves. Industrial types are also made, for furnaces, heaters, etc.

Solid-State Ignition
For Lawnmowers

Everything's going solid-state now—even the lawnmowers! This also includes snowmobiles, small garden tractors, and outboard motors—anything powered by small gasoline engines. For a typical example, here's the system used in the Lawn-Boy mowers, in their 1973 line. It is actually a capacitor-discharge ignition system, self-powered in the same way as the old magneto systems. There are no moving parts in the system itself; no breaker points, no "condenser," etc.

Figure 27-1 is a schematic diagram of the whole system. Three coils are used. One is the charging coil (2), another is the trigger coil (5), and the last is the spark coil (7), which is the same as that used on automobiles. Output of this system is up around 30 kV.

All coils are energized by a magnet built into the rim of the flywheel. As the flywheel turns, the magnet moves past the laminated cores of the coils. Figure 27-2 shows how the unit and magnet are mounted.

Here is the sequence of events which happen as the flywheel turns. When the magnet passes the charge-coil laminations, it induces a voltage in that coil. This is true ac, since the magnetic field is built up, then collapses to make the current reverse. The ac voltage is fed to a diode rectifier (3), converted to dc, and then fed to the capacitor (4) to charge it to about 300 volts.

The other plate of the capacitor is connected to the anode of the silicon controlled rectifier (6). The SCR cathode is connected to the primary winding of the spark coil (7). The SCR's gate is connected to the trigger coil (5). When the magnet passes the trigger-coil lamination, it generates a

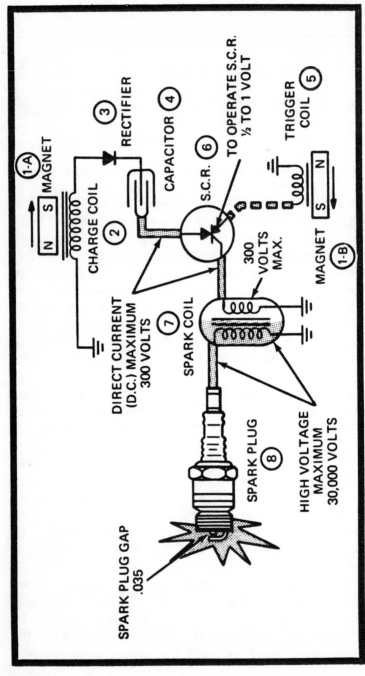

Fig. 27-1. Components of the solid state unit. Numbers are explained in text.

small voltage, only 1 volt or so. This gates the SCR on, and the capacitor is discharged through the spark coil. The high voltage in the secondary fire the spark plug (8).

There's some very clever engineering here! Due to the special design of the flywheel magnets and core laminations, this system has an automatic spark retard. This makes it easier to start (anyone who has ever cranked a Model T Ford with the spark advanced knows why). An automatic retard of about 9 degrees is achieved by this design. After the engine has caught, and run up to speed, anywhere from 800 rpm on up, the system automatically advances the spark by about 29 degrees, which makes the engine run much better.

A "kill" switch grounds the CD system to stop the engine. This is connected through the ignition switch. This switch is used, even on hand-cranked models, for safety. It must be turned on before you can start the engine.

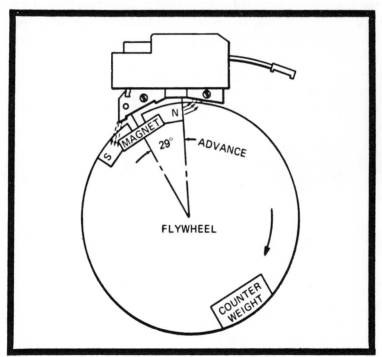

Fig. 27-2. Mechanical detail, showing how magnet advances spark with increasing speed.

Troubleshooting these systems is very simple. They're purely Aristotelian; they work, or they don't! To test the system, take out the spark plug (and check it or clean it, or replace it; plugs cause most of the trouble in all small engines). Clip the spark plug lead to it again, and ground the shell, preferably with a dual clip lead, to the engine. Turn the ignition switch on, and crank the engine. You should get a hot, fat blue spark across the plug's electrodes. If you don't, pull the kill-switch lead, and make sure it isn't grounded. (It has a push-on connector on the ignition switch.) If you still get no spark, the CD unit could be bad. Replacement is simple; only two screws hold it after you take off the air baffle, which has only three screws.

If the module must be replaced, you'll have to use a special nonmetallic gage to get it spaced properly with respect to the flywheel. Without this, the flywheel magnets will pull the laminations against the outside of the flywheel. Clearance at one end is 10 mils, and about ¼ inch at the other. This odd spacing is the key to proper operation of the solid-state system.

Caution: if the engine has been running, don't mess around with the spark plug for at least 10 seconds! Just allow the CD charge to leak off.

Limit Switches

There's one handy safety device that you'll find on a lot of heating appliances. It should be used on all of them, really. This may look like an odd-shaped blob with several wires going into it. It's called a **limit** switch. It is a switch, automatically operated by a thermal element, usually a bimetal blade. It's normally closed. When the temperature of the appliance heater reaches a certain level, the switch opens, to keep things from getting too hot. In some of the larger units, the bimetal blade may be in the form of a spiral or coil, instead of the familiar flat blade, but it works in the same way.

Many of these are adjustable. You will see a calibrated scale, marked in degrees (F). A sliding pointer shows the cutoff temperature for which it is set. Some of these have locking screws; if the pointer can't be moved, look for a small screw that holds it in place. Loosen this, and then retighten it after adjusting the switch. Some types are preset; these open the switch at a certain temperature.

On a gas furnace or similar heater, with a fan to force air flow, the limit switch may be a dual type. One section will control the fan motor. This stays open until the plenum has reached a high temperature; this keeps the fan from blowing cold air up your pants-legs. The other section is the limit-switch. It is usually actuated by the same thermal element, but it is normally closed.

The power to the electrically operated main gas valve flows through these contacts. If the temperature of the plenum goes too high, they open, and the gas valve automatically

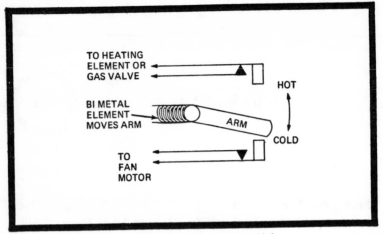

Fig. 28-1. Gas valve limit switch.

closes. Standard gas valves are built so that when the power fails, they close automatically (Fig. 28-1). This type of dual switch will have two pointers; one sets the temperature at which the fan comes on, the other the temperature at which the burner is cut off.

Some of these switches use the familiar flat blades, with electrical contacts in an insulated mounting on the ends. In the heavy-duty types, such as those found on furnaces, the switch itself may be a Miroswitch or similar unit. These take only a very small pressure to operate; they are tripped by an arm on the end of the thermal blade or spiral unit.

Other types can be found in the heating ducts of electric or gas clothes dryers. These are generally preset, fixed types. Their purpose is to prevent the temperature in the duct from going too high. A typical unit might close at about 200 degrees and open at 300-350 degrees; this varies with different units. If a control shorts, or anything happens that would let the heating element stay on too long, this thermostat opens, breaking the supply circuit. A similar control can be used with gas heated dryers. If the duct temperature goes too high, the limit switch shuts off the main gas valve.

In most clothes dryers, there will be another thermostat in series with the limit switch. This one works just like the limit switch, of course, but it will be adjustable for various temperatures, so that the dryer can be used with different kinds of fabrics. Some models have as many as 6 different heats.

The thermostats used for this purpose, in clothes dryers, will look quite a bit different to the types found on furnaces, etc. They'll be small round-cased units, with lugs or push-on terminals. Many of these are of the disc type. They're bimetal, just like the blade, but made in the form of a dished disc. When this gets hot, it will snap from one side to the other, just like the bottom of an oilcan! This operates the electrical contacts.

CHECKING AND SERVICING

Finagle's First Law says, "If there is anything in there that can cause trouble, it certainly will!" So, if any kind of heating unit refuses to work, check the fuel supply first—gas or electricity. If this is present at the normal value, then check the gas burner or electric heating element. If you can read the full supply voltage across the terminals of an electric heating element, but it's stone cold, the element is open. Replace with an exact duplicate.

However, if your check at the terminals of the heating element shows zero voltage, then you've got another problem! Something between the line plug and the heating element is open. Incidentally, one good thing to check here is to be sure that the thing is turned on! Check the timer, switch, or whatever turns it on.

In large appliances such as clothes dryers, it's usually not too difficult to follow the wiring; it's visible. The thermostats, etc. will be fairly easy to see. Take a voltage reading right across the terminals of the thermostats and switches. Full line voltage present across what should be a closed switch indicates trouble. One quick check for this is to turn it off, connect a jumper across the suspected switch, etc. and apply power. If the unit starts to heat, run, etc., turn it off and replace that thermostat or switch.

In the plastic-cased thermostats, switches, etc., check the terminals. They should be clean, and tight in the body of the unit. In quite a few cases, the switch contacts can overheat, cause the body of the switch to char, and make the terminal come loose! This is a dandy cause of intermittent operation of the appliance. It will work perfectly one time, then refuse to go at all the next. Wiggle wiring, and check terminals, etc. Something is loose, not making good tight contact.

Careful attention to small details can help you find and fix some otherwise puzzling problems. Check everything!

Modular Appliances

Everything is "going modular" these days—including appliances. One major appliance manufacturer has brought out a line of small household electric appliances which can actually be taken apart and put back together without tools! The parts are designed in subassemblies or modules which snap in, plug in, or are latched in place.

This line includes four of the most common units, so far—a toaster, toaster-oven, electric percolator, and wonder of wonders (at least to those of us who have struggled to get the things apart for so long), an electric iron!

The iron is built in five major units; the sole plate, which includes the thermostat, the plastic water reservoir, the handle, the spray assembly, and the line cord. To take it apart, start with the cord. Slide a latch aside, and the cord comes out (see Fig. 29-1A). Next comes the handle unit. A release lever knob under the reservoir unit is moved, and the whole handle lifts up and off (Fig. 29-1B).

The reservoir can then be taken off the handle unit, by pushing down on one end and sliding it out (C). The spray pump and filter assembly then comes off by lifting it up and away (D). To put it back together, just go through these steps in reverse order and there you are.

All of the standard tests can be used. As usual, most of the electrical troubles will be in the line cord. This is due to the normal flexing while in use. If the cord checks open, a replacement unit can be plugged in. The cord, by the way, can be changed from side to side, for the convenience of left-handed or right-handed users. Just reverse the plug on the handle.

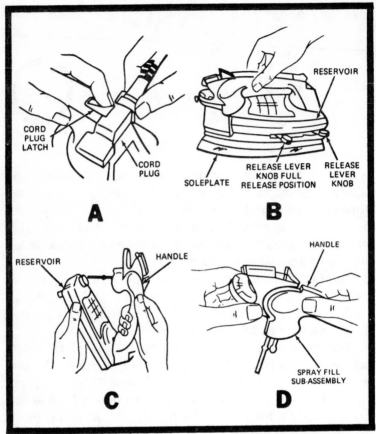

Fig. 29-1. Proctor-Silex modular steam iron.

The spray pump (steam unit) is another common source of trouble. This is frequent in areas where tap water has a fairly high mineral content. When the water is heated to steam, it may leave a hard mineral deposit which clogs up the tiny holes in the spray pump or drip nozzle. The makers have thoughtfully included a spare rubber valve cap, and even a short piece of cleaning wire, just the right size for opening up the hole in the spray pump nozzle! (Which is great, for I never have a piece of wire of just the size I want.)

If the drip valve in the plastic reservoir clogs up so that the water doesn't drip into the steam unit (the sole plate) this can sometimes be cleaned with the wire. The use of distilled water will help to avoid this problem in hardwater areas. This is available at drugstores and auto supply stores, in bottles of several sizes.

The "modular percolator" is made in seven units, which include all of the pieces inside the bowl—the coffee basket, lid, etc. The heating element is a sealed unit, locked inside the plastic base.

The heating element is designed so that it can be replaced by simply turning a locking knob on the underside of the base. A special bracket is used on the element; it cannot be taken out unless the appliance plug is removed. This eliminates any possibility of electrical shock to the repairman or user. If the element is bad, a new one is simply slipped into place, and the locking knob turned to the "closed" position.

The toaster units are made in the same way. All parts can be removed by lifting latches or levers. The toaster-oven is a combination pop-up toaster and table oven, made in the same way. All parts can be taken off and put back without tools.

Complete, well illustrated instructions and service manuals come with each unit. The complete disassembly and reassembly process is illustrated, so that even the novices can do the job. This should make life quite a bit easier for the home handyman. However, he won't have any excuse left, not even the original one about "I can't find my favorite screwdriver!"

30 Plug-In "Refrigerator Analyzer"

General Electric's major appliance division has come up with a real timesaver for refrigerator technicians. "Plug-in test adapters" have been used by electronics technicians for a long time. The best known are the little socket test adapters, plugged into tube sockets, with the tube in a socket on top. This makes all terminals easily accessible for measurement, in normal operation.

General Electric's "R-E-D" test unit (Rapid Electrical Diagnosis) is a very simple but very useful device. It's just a little "jack box," with switches, a pilot light, and a pair of cables with 9-pin Molex connectors. All of the late-model GE refrigerators are equipped with a plug-socket combination in the main control wiring cable. This is brought out to the front

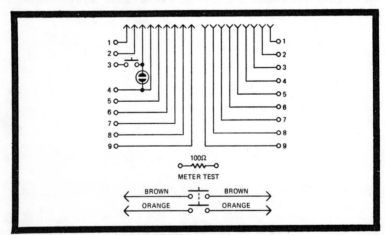

Fig. 30-1. GE refrigerator analyzer.

of the cabinet, at the bottom. These are separated, and the R-E-D tester plugged in. This "fans out" the entire electrical circuitry of the refrigerator. Each lead is brought out to one of the pin jacks, numbered to correspond to the plug terminals. In this condition, all circuits are open.

A pilot light on the panel shows whether ac power is getting to the unit or not. Power should be turned off, by turning the temperature control off, before the R-E-D unit is plugged in. If the light doesn't light, the house fuse may be open, there may be a loose lead in the cable, or the line plug may have been pulled from the outlet. The line voltage can be read at terminals 3 and 4. A schematic of the test unit is in Fig. 30-1.

At the bottom of the panel (see Fig. 30-2) a switch has its four terminals brought out to test leads with pin plugs. By

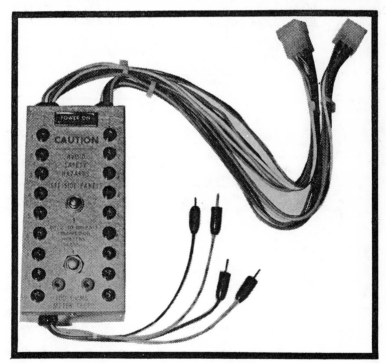

Fig. 30-2. The refrigerator analyzer checks the refrigerator's controls and components through connectors behind a bottom/front panel. Test leads are for ohmmeter resistance checks. (Courtesy Robinaire Mfg. Co.)

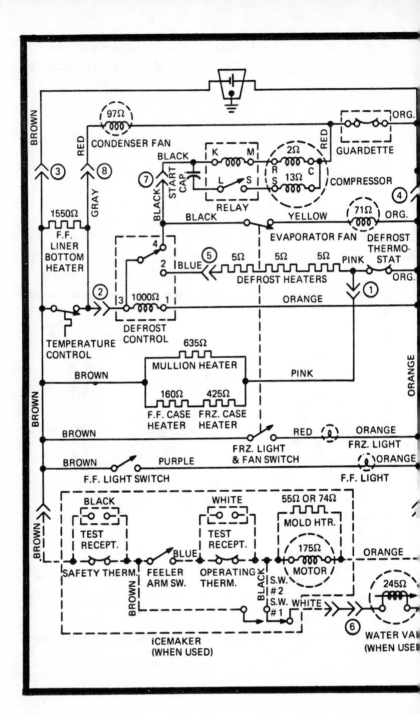

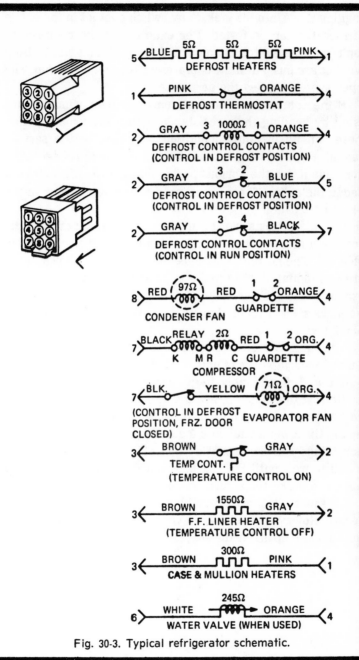

Fig. 30-3. Typical refrigerator schematic.

133

plugging these into the jacks, any switch contact in the entire refrigerator can be tested. For example, if the compressor won't run, the switch is connected to No. 3 and No. 7. Both switches are pushed; if the compressor is okay, it will run. The upper switch applies the ac power.

If the compressor does not run, the motor windings are tested by reading their resistance across the proper jacks. These can be instantly identified by checking the service manual. Figure 30-3 is a schematic of a typical refrigerator. Alongside it are the various parts, showing the pin numbers used in the cable. These correspond to the numbering on the R-E-D unit panel.

Ohmmeter tests can be made on switch contacts, thermostats, motor windings, heating elements, and electric valve solenoids. The normal resistance of each will be shown in the service manual. Just to make assurance doubly sure, a test resistor of 100 ohms is included in the R-E-D unit, across the two jacks seen at the bottom of the panel. These are marked meter test.

This unit can save a great deal of time, especially in making accurate tests of units that would otherwise take a lot of time and disassembly to get at.

Defrost thermostats, heating elements, and many others are hard to locate. You can operate most of them by connecting the lower switch into the circuits; defrost heaters and such things can be turned on and off and checked without having to wait until the box has cooled down or warmed up enough to make them turn on normally.

This unit will check everything except the little light inside the box! However, if you have a very small helper, this is easy. Just shut him up inside the box, and he can tell.

Transistor Testing

One fellow says, "An ohmmeter's not worth a darn for transistor testing! I like a curve-tracer."

Another one says, "Nay, nay. In-circuit beta tester is the only thing that'll give you good results!"

The truth of the matter is that almost any kind of test equipment will give you some results in transistor testing. It depends on how you use it and how you interpret the results. There's no such thing as a universal tester for solid-state stuff.

The first and probably the most frequently used is the ohmmeter. You can get a lot of dope in a hurry with an ohmmeter. The No. 1 test is strictly a "bang-bang" check on any medium-resistance range. Take a reading from any element to any other; then reverse the prods. This reverses the polarity of the ohmmeter battery (Fig. 31-1). So you get a low resistance reading (forward-biased junction) one way, and a high-resistance reading (back-biased junction) the other.

Due to the wide variation of transistor resistances, and the difference in ohmmeter battery voltages, there's no such thing as a standard resistance. So, all you need to look for is "high one way, low the other." Very low or zero resistance both ways—it's shorted. Or there is something shunted across it in the circuit under test.

Check the schematic, if available. If not, yank the transistor out and recheck. If you get this kind of reading out-of-circuit, it is shorted.

Don't set the ohmmeter on too high a range. The x100 scale is a good compromise setting. On a batch of typical tran-

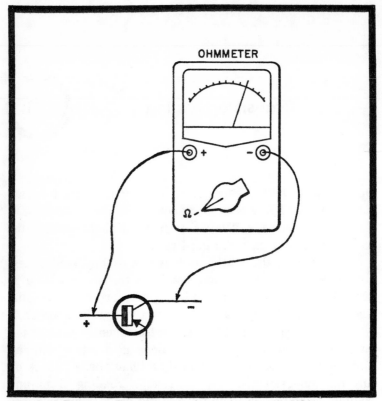

Fig. 31-1. Transistor electrode checks with VOM.

sistors, I got low readings from 1000 ohms to 5000 ohms, and 15K, 60K on high. You hear repeated warnings about using an ohmmeter on transistors, for fear of blowing the transistor with the ohmmeter battery voltage. I won't say it can't happen, but it has never happened to me. Possibly the series resistance inside the ohmmeter limits the current to a very low value. It's current which blows transistors. (Better not use your ohmmeter on an IC, though—not unless you know the VOM's batteries are well within the IC's tolerance.

One thing you do need to know is the polarity of your ohmmeter battery. In many older VOMs and some VTVMs, the red lead was always negative. Most late models have the red lead positive. If you know which is which, you can find out the sex of any transistor with a simple test.

Put the ohmmeter negative lead on the base. If this is a pnp device, you'll read a low resistance to both collector and emitter. Reversing the prods; high resistance to both. If it's an npn, putting the positive lead to the base will give you low resistance to collector and emitter. Reverse the prods; both high. You automatically check for internal shorts at the same time, of course.

MEASURING LEAKAGE

Now comes the real bugaboo—leaky transistors. In germanium transistors, a small amount of leakage is okay. With silicons, so popular now in rf, i-f, and even af stages—none. Zero!

Leakage must be read with the transistor out-of-circuit and on an accurate leakage tester. Any of the better modern transistor testers will read it.

Leakage problems show up in TV agc, direct-coupled audio amplifiers, rf amplifiers, and so on. Transistor bias is always critical, but there seem to be quite a few stages where it's supercritical. And if you think 10 mA leakage isn't a heck of a lot, put one with this much leakage into an agc stage and watch the fur fly!

You should never grab a transistor tester, ohmmeter, or anything like that and jump in checking transistors at random. This is a waste of time. As far as I can see from quite a bit of bench testing of test methods, we're probably going to have to go back to signal tracing!

This started in the late 1930s. There were quite a few specialized test instruments built for just this purpose. In fact, if you happen to have an old Hickok Trace-O-Meter or Meissner Analyst under your bench, blow the dust off it.

The idea of this is very simple. We need to know where the signal stops. That's where we start our testing. The part causing trouble is either in this stage or one of the stages which control it.

This brings up another highly useful instrument—the oscilloscope. Using it, and any kind of signal source—even a broadcast signal—you can get into the area of the trouble in far less time than with any other test instrument. You can feed any kind of identifiable signal into the input of the device and go through the circuit until you find the point where the signal stops.

Any kind of signal is useful. You can check out a video amplifier stage with a record player and an audio test record if you want to.

One good quick-check for normal operation, very useful in places like transistor i-f stages, and any stage using the popular common-emitter circuit, is the emitter voltage. There will almost always be an emitter resistor, and the voltage drop across this is a good clue.

If the emitter voltage is normal, the transistor is conducting normally. Zero emitter voltage means the transistor is either cut off or completely open. Abnormally high emitter voltage means the transistor is either conducting very heavily, or is shorted. Either one means trouble.

In stages where the bias varies quite a bit with an input signal, be sure to check the schematic to see exactly how this voltage is measured—with signal or no-signal. This can make a great difference in agc, i-f, sync, or even audio stages.

Test Instrument Tricks 32

You can do a lot of things with "standard" test equipment. Use your imagination. For example, here are some typical questions:

"How can I measure the value of a 4000 uF electrolytic, when my capacitor-checker only goes to 2000 uF?"

Disconnect it, and connect another one in series with it (Fig. 32-1), watching polarity. If the other one is also 4000 uF, the combination is now a 2000 uF unit and you can read it. If the extra one is, say, 1000 uF the resultant capacitance will be somewhere around 800 uF. The total value of series capacitances is the reciprocal of the sum of the reciprocals:

$$\frac{1}{\frac{1}{C1} + \frac{1}{C2} + \frac{1}{C3}, \text{etc.}}$$

If you have only two values, it's even simpler, like this:

$$\frac{C1 \times C2}{C1 + C2} = \text{TOTAL}$$

By the way, you can use the reverse of this to check a very small capacitor, if it comes out jammed right up to one end of the dial. Connect a known capacitor across the terminals of the checker (take the test leads off). Balance for the widest eye-opening or meter deflection, whichever yours does. Now connect the unknown across this one, and rebalance the bridge. You can usually read 3- to 4 pF capacitors by the increase in reading needed to restore balance.

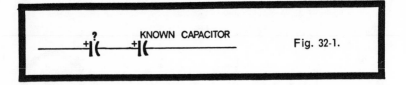

KNOWN CAPACITOR

Fig. 32-1.

Cable Breaks

"I've got a long shielded audio cable and it's open! Is there an easy way to find out where the break is?"

Yep. Leave the capacitor checker turned on! Connect it right across one end of the cable, from inner conductor to shield. Balance the bridge and note the capacitance reading. This is the capacitance between the inner conductor and the shield. Actual reading isn't important.

Now go to the other end of the cable and repeat this test. Most cables break right at one end or the other, at the plugs. If you get a good-sized capacitance reading at one end, and practically nothing at the other, the very low-reading end is where the break is (Fig. 32-2).

If the two readings are almost the same, the break is somewhere near the center of the cable. For example; cable with 1.0 pF capacitance per foot, and 100 ft long. You read 60 pF at one end and 40 pF at the other. The break is 60 ft from the

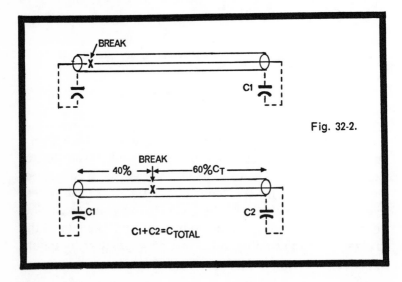

Fig. 32-2.

60 pF end. (Notice how I make those figures come out even?) In actual cables it won't come out so even, of course, but the percentage will!

Take the two readings and add them. This is the total capacitance of the cable. Now measure the length, and you'll get the capacitance per foot. Do the mathematics and you'll find out where the break is from either end, in terms of the percentage of total length. (Incidentally, this is handy for checking out long rolls of shielded cable, coax, etc. on a reel without unwinding the whole thing. In fact, you can even use this method between a good wire and a broken one—inside an intercom cable, etc. Read the capacitance between the known good wire and the broken ends.

"They tell me that the circuit breaker pops at 1.25A ac. I haven't got an ac ammeter! How can I read it?"

Use a genuine simplified Ohm's law digital computer! In other words, connect a good 1-ohm resistor in series with the circuit. Then connect an ac voltmeter across the resistor (Fig. 32-3). Now, each 1V ac read on the meter indicates 1 ampere of current flowing through the resistor. Count it up on your fingers (that's where the "digital computer" comes in).

This same gadget can be used to read milliamperes, in high voltage dc circuits. Just use a good 1000 ohm resistor. For every milliampere of current flowing through the resistor, you read 1.0 volts ac or dc; just be sure to use a high-impedance meter.

The same trick will work in low-voltage dc circuits, but you can't use a 1-ohm resistor, especially down around 6 volts or so. One ampere of current will cause a 1.0-volt drop across the resistor, and your set will have only 5.0 volts left! You can use this if you have a variable-output dc bench power supply. Just run the voltage up until you read the correct input voltage at the set. This will compensate for the metering-resistor drop and everything will be normal.

"How can I read the rf output of a little CB transmitter on my scope? I get nothing, just a line."

That's normal. The average service scope doesn't have much sensitivity at 27 MHz! So you're not going to get a heck

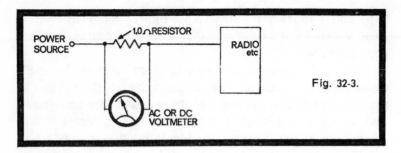

Fig. 32-3.

of a lot of signal through your vertical amplifier. Connect a diode across the direct-probe tip, and then modulate the CB transmitter with some kind of audio signal. For example, feed an audio oscillator to a little speaker; tie the push-to-talk button of the CB transmitter down, and place the mike close to the speaker cone. Then look for the tone-modulating frequency on the scope.

If you have a crystal-demodulator probe with your scope, use it. If the pattern isn't high enough, fasten about 12 to 15 inches of wire to the probe tip and couple it loosely to the transmitter's whip antenna. If you must make tuning adjustments, etc. tune for maximum pattern height. Incidentally, a No. 222 penlight bulb makes a good "dummy antenna" for very small CB transmitters. Won't glow very brightly, but will glow enough to be sure that the thing is putting out rf. Solder the bulb to regular antenna plug used on set. Remove antenna.

There are lots of other ways to use your "common" test equipment, to make special tests. Use your ingenuity! You'll come up with lots of useful ideas. Have fun!

Phono Amplifier Totem Pole

Practically all hi-fi or stereo systems today are solid state. The most popular output circuit seems to be the output-transformerless type—either complementary-symmetry or "stacked" circuit. This is sometimes called a "totem pole" because the transistors are schematically stacked on to of each other. Figure 33-1 (one channel of the GE T2N4 stereo phonograph) shows a simple type of stacked circuit. Both transistors are of the same polarity, npn.

Because of the direct connections between transistors, they can be hard to check out unless you use the right methods. Note that Q4 is connected from base to base of Q6-Q8, the outputs. The emitter of Q2 is directly connected to the base of Q4. (And this is one of the simple ones!)

If the amplifier is completely dead on both channels, check the dc power supply voltages first. If these are okay, then read the dc voltages from top to bottom of the totem pole. The key voltage in this circuit is the dc voltage on the emitter-of-Q6, collector-of-Q8 junction.

This is the no-signal voltage. Without an input signal, these dc voltages should divide up as they are shown here: +15V on the collector of Q6, and +5.4V on the emitter-collector junction. This voltage will tell you what's happening. If you get zero volts here, but the full +15V on Q6's collector (supply voltage), Q6 is either open or completely cut off. (The last can be quickly checked by reading Q6 base voltage.) This is normally unlikely; it would take quite a bit of negative voltage on the base to cut Q6 off, and there's no place for it to come from in this circuit! The chances are that Q6 collector-emitter junction is open.

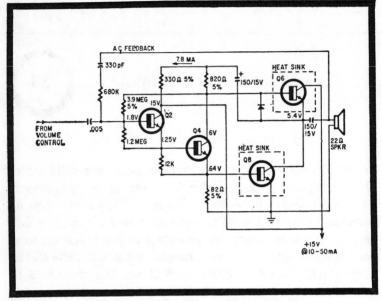

Fig. 33-1. GE T2N4 stereo phono channel.

The actual voltage ratio between top collector, center junction, etc. will vary with different makes. Some will split it evenly, others will have an unequal division, as here. In any case, it should be pretty close to the ratio given on the schematic.

The GE model T20E (Fig. 33-2) has a more powerful amplifier circuit, with more elaborate interconnections, in these, or in any circuit where one transistor is connected "across" another, you'll have to break the circuit before you can get a reliable test. Even the best in-circuit transistor testers won't read a transistor correctly like this. To get a handle on this type of circuit, take out the middle transistor. This leaves both of the end ones ready for tests. (Then you usually find that the one you just took out and laid on the bench was the bad one.)

If the complaint is distortion in one or both channels, there's only one really quick way to find the cause. Feed in a good clean audio signal, anywhere around 500-1000 Hz. Then follow this with a scope. You will be able to see any problems.

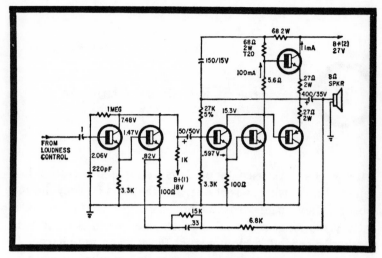

Fig. 33-2. GE T20E phonograph channel.

Be sure you aren't overloading the input. You can make up a homemade voltage divider with a couple of resistors to be sure that the input signal isn't too high. Rule of thumb: not more than 1V peak to peak.

Check the signal at the input, then at the output of the first stage. If you show peak clipping of the sine wave here, cut down the input signal.

Once you find the point where the signal either stops or distorts, you can take dc voltage readings, test transistors and check resistors.

Small leakages in transistors can cause large distortions. (They upset the bias.)

34   The SCR Battery Charger

Battery chargers used to be fairly simple devices; a low voltage transformer, a rectifier, and that was it. They did the job, but they could also do some damage. Leave one on a battery too long, and you're in trouble. When a battery is partly discharged, a high current flows when the charger is hooked up. As the battery charges, this current decreases. However, if the charger is left hooked up after the battery has reached full charge, some current will still be flowing. The actual amount depends on the voltage of the charger and its current rating.

This current doesn't do any useful work, since the battery is already up to full charge. What it does is generate heat. This makes the water evaporate out of the electrolyte, and it also liberates gases which can be dangerous. (Oxygen plus hydrogen plus small spark makes one heck of a bang!)

So the newer chargers are provided with a voltage-sensing circuit. This turns the charger off when the battery reaches full charge. The "signal" for this is the voltage across the battery. Before it reaches full charge, this will be lower than normal; when it is fully charged, it will rise.

Automatic protection is provided by an SCR, in a novel circuit (see Fig. 34-1). As you can see, the transformer and rectifiers are still there. The positive terminal of the dc output (centertap of the transformer) is connected to the anode of the SCR. The negative terminal of the dc output is the common anodes of the rectifiers. So now the charging current flows through the SCR.

An SCR will not conduct current at all, until it is "gated on" by applying a small positive voltage to its gate. Once it is

146

turned on, however, it keeps on conducting until the anode voltage drops to zero. If we look at this as a dc circuit, the SCR would conduct at all times, once turned on. However, this isn't precisely a pure dc circuit. The voltage applied to the SCR anode isn't really dc, but a series of pulses, positive-going. So the SCR turns off every time this voltage reaches zero, which it does 120 times a second. The waveform of this is shown in Fig. 34-1, just above the SCR anode.

So the SCR will actually turn itself off 120 times per second, then be gated back on again for the next half-cycle, by the voltage from the gate-voltage divider. Current will keep flowing into the battery as long as the gate circuit is working.

Three resistors are connected across the output. They actually "read" the dc battery voltage. As the battery charges, this goes more positive. The current through the sensing resistors also increases, as Mr. Ohm said. Now we come to the secret; notice that one of these resistors isn't a

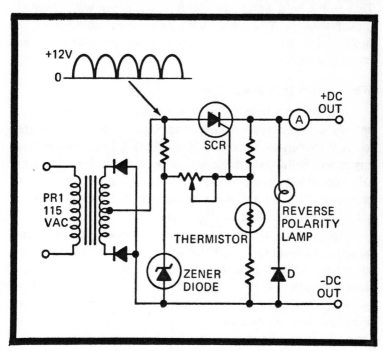

Fig. 34-1. Automatic battery charger.

fixed type, but a thermistor. This is a special type of resistor. When the current flowing through it increases, its resistance decreases. This change is actually caused by the resistance element heating up. That's why the term thermistor.

Now then: when we begin the charge, the battery voltage is comparatively low. The dc voltage drop across the sensing resistors is such that the gate of the SCR stays positive with respect to its cathode; enough to make sure that the SCR stays on. When the battery gets to full charge, the dc voltage rises. So the current through the sensing resistors rises with it. In fact, this current rises slightly more than it would if all of these were standard resistors. This is because of the reduced resistance of the thermistor, with increased current.

Its resistance drops; so does the voltage drop across the bottom section of the divider. This results in the SCR gate becoming not quite positive enough to be turned on. So, it blocks current flow, and the battery will not be overcharged. This won't be a complete cutoff. The meter will generally flicker slightly. The zener diode and the resistor across the supply also help out in this action by providing a fixed reference voltage.

What To Do If It Doesn't Work

The old standard test that we used to make to see if a battery charger was working, was popping the clips together to see if there was a spark. I don't think I'd recommend this any more. Solid-state devices dislike any transients, so don't take chances. In most of these chargers, you will have a panel ammeter. This will tell you whether any current is flowing or not. Connect the clips to the battery.

Many of these chargers have a clever little reverse-polarity indicator circuit, which tells you if you have managed to connect the battery up backward. This is the diode and lamp shown across the dc output. If the battery is hooked up correctly, the cathode of the diode has a positive voltage applied to it. It won't conduct. If the battery polarity is reversed, the cathode will have a negative voltage on it. It will go into full conduction, and the lamp will light brightly. Connected as this circuit is, the meter needle will back off-scale if the battery is reversed. This will be only the lamp current, and won't hurt anything. If the lamp lights, but the meter is reading upscale, the diode is shorted!

If the ammeter needle doesn't move when the battery is connected, the first thing to do is check to see if the line cord is plugged in. In this type of regulated charger, as I said before, even if the battery should happen to be fully charged, the ammeter needle will flicker slightly if it's working.

If it doesn't move at all, though the line cord is plugged in, check for an open fuse or circuit breaker inside the charger. If these all check out, the SCR could be open, or is not being gated on. This can be checked by simply jumpering the SCR with a clip-lead. If current flows now, something is wrong with the SCR or its circuitry.

This will have to be checked out with a dc voltmeter. The SCR gate should be slightly positive with respect to its own cathode. It takes only about +0.4 volt to turn the average SCR on. You can take the SCR out and check it. A shorted SCR will read zero with ohmmeter prods either way.

If the charger works but the current is very low, one of the diodes could be open. This will show you an open circuit, with prods either way, across the bad diode. A normal diode reading is a very low resistance one way and a very high resistance with the ohmmeter prods reversed.

35

Ignition Problems
In Small Engines

My wife couldn't start the mower we had, though she loved to run it. So I got a nice electric-start rider. Now, Ol' Dad could sit in the living room and watch the football game, while Mom taxied happily around the yard. There was one severe hitch in the git-along, though. The ignition system on the new job radiated electromagnetic energy like crazy! Tore up every TV channel!

After some head-scratching, I decided that the simplest thing was the best, at least for a start. So, I checked the type of spark plug it used, which was an AC No. 45. I hypered into town and got a resistor type replacement, which is an R45. Installing this cleaned up the ignition noise very nicely.

For the benefit of those old mechanics who think that this type of plug upsets the ignition, let me say that I ran a long series of tests on cars, a long time before resistive ignition wire became the standard. It has absolutely no effect on either the starting or running. If the ignition system is in shape to run at all, resistor plugs or resistive wiring won't bother it a penny's worth.

This will work in the magneto ignition systems of other engines as well. These don't seem to cause as much trouble with TVI as the electric systems, but if they do, it would be a good starting point. For those who have one with this type of engine, which includes all of the pull-start types, here's a very good hint: If the engine gets hard to start, the first thing to do is replace the spark plug. You ought to have a spare tucked away in the garage!

If you're in a hurry and don't want to run to town and get a new plug, try this: Take the old plug out and close the gap on the points. When these plugs have been used for too long, some of the metal of the points burns away, widening the gap. Tap the movable point gently with a screwdriver handle, etc. until it is very close: 0.025 inch is about right. (If you want a handy gap gage which will always be with you, the average male thumbnail will be very close to 0.025.)

For a quick check of the ignition system, take the plug out, but leave it hooked to its wire. Lay it on the engine, and pull the starter. If you can see a pretty bright blue spark, your ignition is okay.

This leads to the next thing; most common offender here is a little water in the gas tank. You can get this from condensation in a partly filled tank. The water will drop to the bottom of the tank; if you take the cap off and look inside (with a flashlight! Not a match, Clyde!), you can usually see what looks like bubbles rolling around on the bottom. In most of these engines, the carburetor picks up the gas through a tiny tube that goes almost to the bottom; so, the first thing it gets is some of the water.

Cure is simple; turn the thing upside down and drain all of the gas and water out. If you can still see some liquid on the bottom afterward, wrap a small (non-lint type) rag on the end of a stick and swab it out until it's dry. Refill with fresh gas and try it.

Magneto Ignition

Just as a refresher, a magneto is a coil, mounted on the engine, and a magnet. The magnet is cast into the inside of the flywheel. When this revolves, the magnet passes the core of the coil. The change in magnetic field generates a high-voltage pulse.

In some engines, you'll find a set of contact points, with a condenser, mounted on top of the engine under the flywheel. These are closed by a tiny spring-loaded plunger which goes into a recess in the shaft. This makes the magneto fire at exactly the right time. This is similar to the distributor on a car, but isn't in the high-voltage circuit at all. The spark plug lead goes from the high-voltage coil directly to the plug.

After long use, these points get dirty. To get at them, you'll have to remove the flywheel and starter assembly. If these contacts are very dirty and pitted, a new set of points and a condenser will do wonders for that hard-starting old engine.

Actual magneto failure is pretty rare. One real whizzer can be found if the magnet loses its strength! This is also rare, but can happen if the flywheel is struck a hard blow right over the magnet, or if it's overheated. For a quick check, hold a screwdriver blade near it. It should be strong enough to pull the blade tip smartly.

Batteries

The batteries used in the electric-start units are small ones, mostly 12V, about the size of a motorcycle battery or smaller. Some makes use a straight 12V dc system. The battery, connected to the starter, cranks the engine. The starter will be gear-driven, so that after the engine starts, it is turned and will act as the generator to recharge the battery.

In the later models, a dual-wound type of unit is used. There is a dc motor winding for starting; there is also an ac alternator winding. You'll usually find a pair of diodes, mounted in spring clips, with leads going to the battery. Caution: in most of these systems, you'll find a warning notice. The battery must be disconnected from the system before recharging with an external battery charger. Failure to do this may blow the diodes. (I'm taking their word for it. When I recharge mine, I disconnect it.)

36

Automatic light switches have become quite popular in rural and suburban areas alike. These use a very simple electronic circuit; a photocell controls a small relay. When the outside light is high enough, the light goes off. Figure 36-1 shows the schematic of a typical unit. This is one of the smaller types, for controlling lamps up to 300 watts. There are several different sizes, including types which can control high-intensity mercury lamps covering large areas.

The alternating current comes in at the top (white) wire, flows through a 5100-ohm resistor(R), through a cadmium sulfide (CdS) photocell, then through the coil of the relay and back to the line. The CdS cell here is used as a variable resistance.

When the cell is dark, it has a high resistance. Light falling on it makes the resistance drop, and more current flows. The relay contacts do the actual switching. They are normally closed (NC); when the relay is **not** energized, the closed contacts keep power going to the lamp. If anything goes wrong in the control circuitry, the light remains lit.

The control unit will usually be mounted on top of the lamp reflector, under a small metal cover. A window in the cover exposes the photocell. For best results, this window should be on the north side of the cover when installed. This keeps the direct rays of the sun from falling on it and gives better control of the light.

To check one of these out, if the lamp won't light, replace the bulb. If that doesn't help, cover the window on the housing with your hand. You should hear the relay click. If this hap-

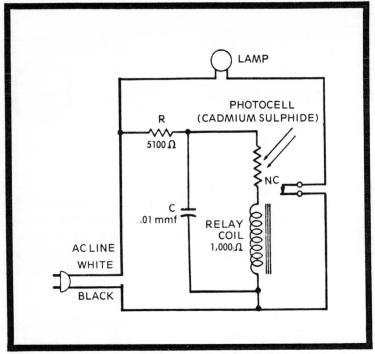

Fig. 36-1. Schematic diagram of small photocell light control unit.

pens, but the light still refuses to go on, turn the power off and remove the cover. There will be several hot wires exposed, so don't take any chances.

Check the relay contacts; they may be burned or pitted so badly that they do not make contact, even though the armature of the relay may pull in. In most of these units, the contacts will be easily accessible. Pull a strip of fine sandpaper between them, holding the armature down with your finger (power OFF, remember!).

Close the relay manually, and look at the contacts; you will be able to tell whether they're touching or not. Turn the power on, keeping clear, and recheck. You can cover the photocell with a piece of dark paper or cloth.

One common cause of damage to these units is a nearby hit from lightning. If this has happened, you will probably be able to see burned parts, charred insulation, or carbon "tracks" across insulators. If this is the case, the unit will have to be taken off and repaired.

Disconnect both wires and remove the control unit and lamp socket. Take it to the bench. You'll need an ohmmeter to check it. Disconnect the capacitor across the relay coil and check it for shorts. If it has shorted, the 5100-ohm resistor will probably be well charred, too. Replace these, if they're bad. Before connecting them back, check the relay coil. If it, too, has been damaged by the lightning, its coil will look very dark, or even charred. Normal resistance of a typical unit will be about 1000 ohms.

Even if the capacitor didn't take a direct hit, its case may have exploded; this sometimes occurs when a high induced voltage is developed across the capacitor. Fortunately, capacitor values aren't too critical; a 0.01 uF capacitor (600V) is a good size.

While the circuit is opened up, check the photocell. With the surface covered, this should read something like 15K or more. Now uncover the cell, let light hit it, and see if the resistance drops to no more than a few thousand ohms. The higher the intensity of light, the lower the resistance. The relay should now close if power is applied to the unit. If it won't move, turn power off, connect a jumper across the photocell, and recheck. The armature should now close unless the coil has some shorted turns.

Figure 36-2 shows the schematic of a larger unit, used with the mercury-vapor lamps. Note the similarity. This one has a temperature-sensitive resistor mounted in shunt with the photocell and coil. Some units have a sensitivity control so that the lamp can be turned on at any desired level of outside light.

The control unit in Fig. 36-1 is practically instantaneous. With the larger units and mercury-vapor lamps, there will be one or two seconds of delay. This isn't due to the control unit; it's the "slow on" characteristic of a mercury-vapor lamp. These are actually "arc lamps," and it takes a little time for the arc to form and "strike."

This delay won't be noticeable in normal operation. However, during a violent thunderstorm, with bright flashes

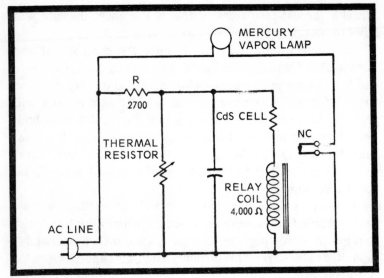

Fig. 36-2. Larger type control unit, for mercury vapor lamps. Bascially same as Fig. 36-1.

of lightning, you may notice the lamp going off. It may stay off for a moment, especially after a very bright flash. The photocells can be temporarily "blocked" by very high-intensity light, just as human vision is temporarily blinded. This won't do any permanent damage—unless, of course, the unit takes a direct hit.

Automatic Coffee Maker

37

The full name of this ubiquitous electrical appliance is "automatic electric coffeemaker with keep-warm provisions," but everybody just says "electric coffeepot." I'd say that it was a tossup as to whether there are more of these in use than electric toasters.

They differ slightly in actual construction, but basically they're a lot alike. They have a heating element, mounted at the bottom of the pot. This is controlled by a thermostat. In the automatic type the full heat stays on until the coffee is brewed. The thermostat then opens, and connects a different heating element in the circuit, in series. This reduces the current, and the temperature, and the coffee stays hot but below the boiling point. The same action also turns on a little neon pilot lamp, signaling "Coffee's ready!"

There isn't a lot to go wrong in one of these. Most of the troubles will be found in the line cord. This has a small appliance plug, fitting the contact pins on the base of the pot. If nothing works, this should be checked first. The heating element or thermostat can open up, but this is pretty rare—unless the thermostat neglected to switch at the end of the perc cycle, in which case an "open" is virtually assured.

The elements are of the metal-sealed type, like the elements used in the electric ranges, and are very durable. The thermostats are also sealed units, of a special type. Figure 37-1 shows an exploded view of a typical coffeemaker of this type.

The thermostat uses a ceramic magnet with some unusual qualities. When it's cold, it's a normal magnet. It pulls the

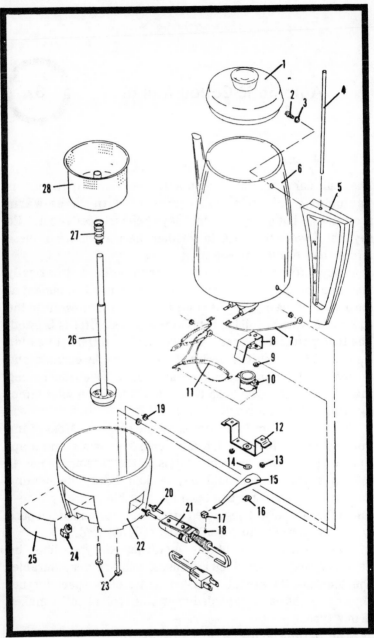

Fig. 37-1. Exploded view of automatic coffee maker. (Courtesy Western Auto Co.)

thermostat contacts together, closing the circuit. When it has been heated up to a given temperature, for a certain period of time, the magnet loses its pull! A small spring opens the contacts. When the magnet has cooled off enough, it regains its magnetism, and closes the contacts once more.

An ingenious method is used to control the brewing time, to make coffee stronger or weaker. The body of the thermostat is mounted on the underside of the pot, held in place by a metal bracket. The main heating element is wound around a small "well" in the bottom of the pot. This concentrates the heat, and starts the "perking" action quicker.

A flange on the thermostat bracket goes over and down along-side one turn of the main element. A small lever coming through the side of the base operates a cam, which is in contact with the flange. Turning the lever toward **strong** moves the flange further away from the element. So the heat takes longer to get to the thermostat, and the coffee brews longer. Moving the flange closer to the element makes the thermostat heat up faster, thus cut off sooner. Figure 37-2 shows a rough sketch of how this works.

Figure 37-3 shows the electrical schematic of this unit. When the pot is plugged in, the thermostat contacts are closed,

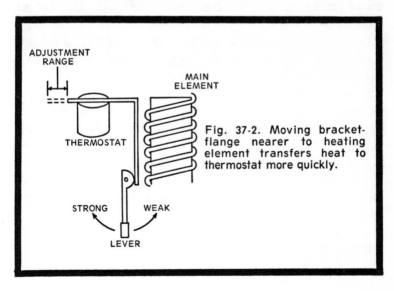

Fig. 37-2. Moving bracket-flange nearer to heating element transfers heat to thermostat more quickly.

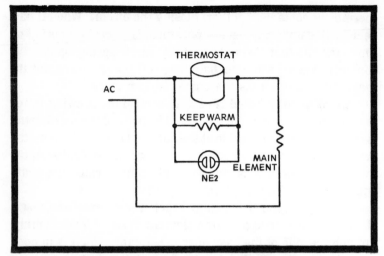

Fig. 37-3. Electrical circuit of coffeemaker.

shorting out the keep-warm element. When the thermostat
operates, the keep-warm element is connected in series with
the main one. So, the current is reduced, and the temperature
goes down. The voltage drop across the keep-warm element is
enough to make the neon lamp light.

Diagnosis of trouble in these is fairly easy. If the coffee
brews normally, but then it gets cold, the main element and
thermostat are okay, but the keep-warm element is open. The
neon pilot light would light, probably quite brightly. If the pot
won't heat at all, check the line cord and appliance plug **first**.
Continuity tests across the line pins on the base will tell you
whether the element is open or not.

In most types of these units, the pot is mounted on a
Bakelite or plastic base; the electrical connections and wiring
will be inside this, for protection. To take the base off the one
in Fig. 37-1, turn it upside down; you'll see two small screws in
the middle. Take these out. There will be a small plastic knob
on the end of the **flavor control** knob. Take this out, and the
knob will slide off.

Next, very carefully work the base loose from the pot.
Take it easy; the wires are usually pretty short, and you'll
break them loose if you're not careful.

Most of the connections will be made with push-on connectors. You can reach inside the base with a pair of long-nose pliers and take these push-on terminals loose for testing. They can be replaced in the same way. The thermostat and other parts will be bolted in place with metal brackets. Be very careful of the leads to the neon lamp. These are pretty small and easy to break. If the worst does happen, this is a standard NE-2 lamp, and it's not too hard to replace.

Final hint: When you're putting it back together, for goodness sake don't drop that little setscrew on the flavor-control knob. If you do, you may be in for a long hunt!

38 Getting Replacement Parts

Getting replacement parts to repair electrical appliances can be quite a headache, if you go at it in the wrong way. With a few simple precautions, it's a lot easier. Luckily for us tinkerers, most of the troubles are in the parts that are universal: line cords, heating elements, and the like. These are obtainable everywhere.

There will be times when you need a special part; something that's used only in this particular make and model. There is really only one "good" source for this: the manufacturer. In the majority of cases, you can get parts from the dealer or distributor specializing in the brand of appliance of interest. If he doesn't have it in stock, he can get it from the maker.

There's one thing that's absolutely essential, to get the part quickly. And to do that you **must** have a complete description of the part. This takes in several items. First is the make and **model number** of the appliance. **Don't** send the **serial number.** This is completely useless! Appliances are listed by model numbers. (In some cases, you'll find two of these.)

Next is a description of the part. You'll be able to use a stock description in most cases; for example, "switch, on-off" or "switch, speed selector," etc. For best results, use the name given in the parts list. To get this, you will need a copy of the service manual for the appliance. Here again, your dealer will be a big help. If you didn't get a copy of this with the appliance, he will have one in his files, and you can look up the part number.

Here's a good example of a typical order:

Item: Blender JC2232.
Model: Factory BL3WIZ
Part: Switch assembly
Number: OBL1 118.

This one is taken from a service data folder for a Western Auto blender. (See Fig. 38-1.) If the dealer doesn't have it in stock, with these names and numbers he can file the order with the nearest parts depot. With this company and many others, you can order directly from the nearest service center, without going through the dealer, if he happens to be a good ways off. Manufacturers have thousands of items on the shelves, and without correct identification, they can't find the right one. So when you get a new appliance, get a copy of the service manual with it. File this with the manuals for all your others.

If you can't locate the factory parts depot, there's still a little hope. There are many appliance "parts houses" around the country. These places carry large stocks of the most frequently needed parts for the standard appliances.

Replacement motors for the smaller appliances can be found readily. If the old motor is burned out, it's generally easier and cheaper to replace it, rather than trying to have the motor rewound. However, many parts supply houses have an "exchange" service for small motors, just like generators and starters on cars. You send them the old motor, and they send you a duplicate, which has been rewound and tested.

Your parts supply house can also be a source for a great many special tools, chemicals, and other things which are essential if you're going to do any amount of appliance work. Get catalogs from all of the places nearest to you. They're handy!

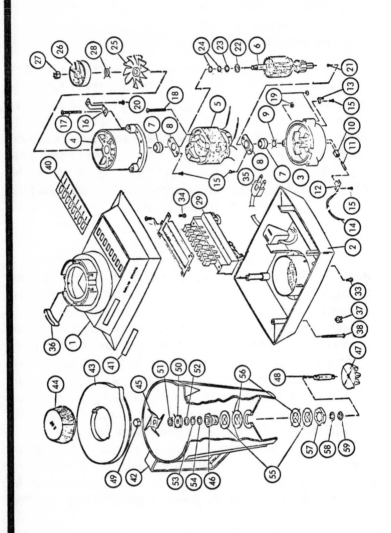

PARTS PRICE LIST

Ref. No.	Part No.	Description	Approx. Sell Price	Ref. No.	Part No.	Description	Approx. Sell Price
1	OBL1 040	Housing, Upper	1.14	31	7000 103	Faston terminal	.03
2	OBL1 002	Housing, lower	1.20	32	7000 049	8/38 Pn Hd screw	.10
3	OBL1 104	Brush housing	.52	33	7000 180	5/16 Ph. screw	.10
4	OBL1 003	End housing	.52	34	7000 046	6/32 Bd hd, screw	.10
5	BLWP5	Stator assembly	2.38	35	OBL1 034	Line cord	.62
6	BL1WPX	Armature assembly	2.64	36	OBL1 016	Boots	.10
7	OOM1 10B	Bearing	.10	37	OBL1 018	Feet	.10
8	OEK7 018	Bearing Retainer	.10	38	7000 177	No. 6BF screw	.10
9	OBL1 027	Thrust Plate	.10	39	OBL1 049	8 x 3/8 screw	.10
10	OBL1 105	Brush	.12	40	7000 041	Switch nameplate	.28
11	OBL1 106	Spring	.10	41	OBL1 112	Nameplate	.12
12	OEK5 221	Brush Holder	.10	42	OBL1 010	Container (Jar)	1.26
13	OEK9 009	Collector Terminal	.10	43	OBL1 005	Container cover	.42
14	OBL1 050	Wire	.62	44	OBL1 006	Measure (Cap)	.12
15	7000 122	4-24 x 1/4 screw	.10	45	OBL1 984	Blade	.60
16	OBL1 059	Bracket	.10	46	BLWP13	Bearing retainer & Bearing assembly	1.18
17	7000 121	8-32 x 1½ screw	.10	47	OBL1 008	Blade driver	.32
18	7000 186	8-32 NC2A M/ screw	.10	48	OBL1 019	Drive shaft	.64
19	7000 009	8-32 Pattern nut	.10	49	7000 184	Cap nut	.10
20	7000 181	6-20 x 3/8 screw	.10	50	OBL1 022	Slinger	.10
21	OBL1 039	Steel ball	.10	51	OBL1 023	Spacer	.10
22	OPFM030	Washer	.10	52	OBL1 024	Neoprene washer	.10
23	7000 160	Thrust washer	.10	53	OBL1 026	Washer shaft seal	.10
24	7000 188	Fibre washer	.10	54	OBL1 025	Phenolic washer	.10
25	OBL1 055	Fan	.20	55	OBL1 013	Washer pressure	.10
26	OBL1 007	Coupling driver	.30	56	OBL1 012	Washer seal	.10
27	7000 185	Hexagon nut	.10	57	7000 179	Palnut No. 5818	.10
28	OBL1 021	Coupling driver	.10	58	OBL1 025	Phenolic washer	.10
29	OBL1 118	Switch assembly	11.68	59	7000 178	Thrust washer	.10
30	OBL1 014	Switch / mt. bkt.	.12				

Fig. 38-1. JC2232 Blender. (Courtesy Western Auto Co.)

Multiple-Speed Electric Fans

Despite the rise in the use of air conditioning, electric fans continue to be very useful and popular. They come in many different shapes and sizes, but they're all alike: a motor turns a propeller to move air. Fans don't look anything like they used to. Instead of the old roundcage type on a pedestal base, they are now mounted in rectangular cases with grilles on each side. Some are single-speed, others have multiple speeds, and some are reversible (the fan will blow either way without your having to turn the case around).

The original speed control on fans was a big wirewound resistor or choke inside the base. This wasted power, and developed quite a lot of heat, making it self-defeating! We're trying to cool off. Later versions use tapped-field motors. Different speeds can be switch-selected, as in Fig. 39-1. The motor can be reversed by means of a similar switch. This is a basic circuit but will match most fans. The motor uses a laminated rotor, with no brushes. The only moving part is the rotor-blade assembly; so, about all the service it needs is an occasional drop of very light oil in the oil holes of the bushings. Don't overdo this; excess oil will drip on the blades and be "slung" off, making the housing messy, attracting lint and dust, and promulgating a familiar oil smell.

The main cause of trouble in these is the selector switch itself. If one of its contacts is dirty, the motor will stop when the switch is in that position.

In most fans, the wires from the motor are attached to the switch with push-on connectors. If the switch gets loose, an attempt to use it causes the switch to turn on the case, pulling all the wires off! Then you must try to locate the proper terminals for the wires.

Actually, this isn't too difficult. You'll probably see that one wire goes directly from the line cord to the motor. This should be the white wire or service ground side. The other side of the ac line goes to one terminal of the switch. The three field tap leads from the motor also go there. But where?

If you have an ohmmeter, connect one side to any one of the switch terminals, and check for continuity to the other three. If you find a reading, turn the switch one position, and check again. Let's say that at first you got a reading from one terminal to the second one around from it. Now, if you get continuity to the third terminal, your ohmmeter lead is on the line terminal, and you're testing to two of the others. This might be L and 2 then 3, as the contacts are numbered in Fig. 39-1. You want to find "L" (line). Keep trying, until you find

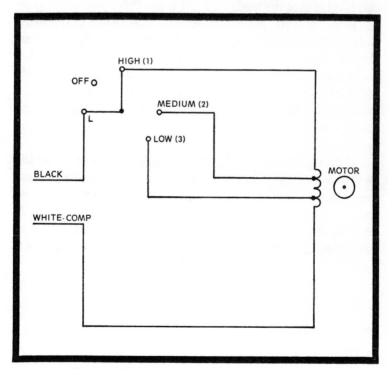

Fig. 39-1. Standard circuit for multispeed fan.

one terminal that can be switched to each of the others in succession.

Connect the black wire from the line to L, and any one of the other leads, from the motor, to No. 2. Now, plug the cord in, and turn the switch until the motor starts. Let's say that this switch is marked "high, medium, low, off" in that order. (Some will be reversed, but the principle's the same.) We've got L, and we need high. If the motor sounds as if the wire we picked was the high speed, check. Pull the plug, take the lead off the switch, and plug another one to the same terminal. Check. Listen to the speed of the blades. This will tell you which wire is the high tap. Put this on terminal 2.

From here on, it's duck soup. Connect the other leads to terminals 3 and 4. Now, switch the fan on, and turn the switch to the three positions. We had high, and it's easy to tell whether medium and low are properly connected. If they're not, just reverse the leads on 3 and 4, and there you are.

Now, get a soft pencil and jot down the colors of the leads on the inside of the fan case for future reference. You may be able to write numbers and L on the body of the selector switch itself. A lot of these are made with a white ceramic body. Note the wire colors, at any rate. Of course, if you want to keep trouble from striking you, you could take the fan apart, and make a note of the colors and positions of the leads on the switch!

If the fan goes dead on one position, this could be either the switch or the tap on the winding. To find out, simply reverse the dead wire and any of the other two. If the fan runs in the position which was dead before, the motor lead is open; if it's dead at the same position, the switch isn't making contact here. Take it apart and clean it; this is possible on many types.

Exhaust Fans 40

One useful electrical appliance that is practically never seen (and ideally, not heard either) is the wall-mounted exhaust fan. Once used almost exclusively in the kitchen, they're found in interior bathrooms, laundry rooms, and at any place where forced ventilation is needed. Figure 40-1 shows a side view of a typical exhaust fan installation.

These are standard electric fans of various sizes. They're mounted in a metal box built right into the wall. The outside is covered by a top-hinged lid to keep rain out. The inside has an ornamental grille. The fan motor is mounted in rubber shock absorbers to hold down the noise. The switch is usually operated by an arm on the outer door; this is lifted by a chain, lever, etc. from inside the house. Since the fan is completely enclosed, no guard cages are needed.

Medium-sized induction motors are used, without brushes. Most motors of this type are lubricated with good sized oil-wicks in the end bells. Very little lubrication is needed; only if the fan sounds draggy or makes noise. When oiling, use a light oil, and put only a few drops in each end.

To get at the fan for checking, take out the long screw usually found in the center of the inside grille. To check for lubrication, spin the blades with your fingers. They should turn freely and "coast" for quite a while. The motor housings of these fans are well sealed, but after long use some fine dust may have gotten in.

If the fan won't run at all, pull the plug; this will be plugged into a special outlet inside the housing. Push the door out to turn the switch on, and check for the presence of ac

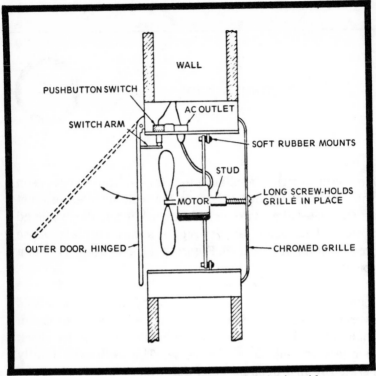

Fig. 40-1. Side view of typical wall-mounted exhaust fan.

voltage in the outlet. If this is dead, check the switch. Push the button several times; listen to the sound. It should make a clean click. If it doesn't, the switch could be dirty. Try squirting some contact cleaner into the edges of the box. Since it would be dangerous to use the fan itself to tell when the switch is working, plug your neon voltage tester into the outlet. Push the switch and watch for the light.

If the switch or outlet must be taken apart, be sure that the power is turned off. If you can get the test light to light up, leave it there, and turn off first one circuit breaker and then another, at the home load center. You'll probably need a "scout" to stand and watch the light, and tell you when it goes out! When you locate the correct breaker, write its number down inside the fan housing! (This should be done **before** you have trouble; saves a great deal of time!)

With the power off, the switch outlet unit can be taken out of the box. If the switch is too dirty to work, it should be replaced. Most of these will use a standard pushbutton, available at electrical supply houses. When any repairs are made or parts replaced inside the junction box, be sure that all wires are well insulated and all connections tight. If wirenuts and pigtails are used, make sure that all leads have the insulation tucked well up inside the body of the connector. If you have any doubts, cover joints with a couple of layers of vinyl electrician's tape, pulled tight.

Exhaust fans in kitchens often pick up quite a coating of grease from cooking vapors. This picks up lint and dust, and can even stick on the fan blades thickly enough to unbalance them. The grille, if it has small openings, can clog up, too. To clean the grille, take it off and wash it in a solvent (NOT gasoline or other flammable liquid).

The easiest way to clean the grille is to make up a dish full of solution with any of the modern laundry detergents. Then, just drop the grille in it, and let it soak for about 15 minutes. This will soften the grease, and it can be brushed off.

While you're waiting for the grille to soak, you can be cleaning the fan blades. The dirt may be scraped off these with a dull knife, and then soaked with detergent on a cloth. Don't use too much, which will make things very messy! If the fan has a heavy accumulation, it can usually be taken out by undoing the mounting bolts. When handling the fan, be sure that you do not bend the blades. This will unbalance the fan and make it noisy.

Before putting the fan back (and every time the fan is inspected and cleaned), check the condition of the line cord from motor to plug. Since the fan runs in fairly hot air and high concentrations of oily vapor, this may have caused a deterioration of the insulation. If you see any signs of cracking in the insulation, take the fan out and replace the line cord. The vibration could cause the cord to hit the housing, resulting in a dangerous short. For safety, these fans should be wired up with the three-wire system.

41   Small Motors

The American household today runs in the middle of a mountain of small electric motors. You don't think so? Take all the motor-driven appliances out in the yard and you'll be surprised at the size of the pile. Let's look at the two most popular types, found in "medium-sized" units; knife-sharpeners, fans, can openers and that ilk.

The simplest one is a **synchronous** motor. It has laminated iron frame, a coil of wire, and an iron rotor. That's all. You'll find these in several shapes, but if you can see that it has only one coil and a solid (actually laminated) rotor, it's a synchronous type. The name comes from the fact that this motor runs at a speed determined by the frequency of the applied ac voltage.

They use miniature versions in electric clocks, and slightly larger ones in medium-sized appliances. Testing this is pretty easy. If it won't run, check to see if the rotor will turn freely. If it will, check for ac voltage at the coil terminals. If you have the voltage, but the motor won't turn, the coil is open.

In many appliances, the coil can be replaced by taking out the bolts that hold the frame together. Then the halves of the frame can be slid out of the coil and the coil can be replaced. You'll have to get an exact duplicate, of course, from the maker of the appliance. (If the frame is riveted together, forget it, Clyde. Get a new motor; they're not that expensive.)

What makes them work? Practically, very simple; theoretically, complex. The varying ac through the coil and frame creates a "twisting magnetic field" which makes the rotor turn (and that's the generalization to end all generalizations, but it's close).

The other type of motor is commonly called a **brush motor**. These are most often built into a cylindrical housing, and have two field coils, and a rotor with coils wound on it. Now we call it an armature. Electrical connection to the armature coils is made through carbon brushes which rest on a cylindrical barrel that is a segmented array of copper bars on one end of the armature. It is a **commutator** (which just means switcher). That's what it does. As the armature turns, it switches a different coil into the circuit.

When power is applied, current flows through the field coil, one of the armature coils, and the other field coil. This creates a magnetic field inside the frame. The magnetic polarity of this field is such that it "pushes" on the armature coil. Since it can move, it does. When this happens, the commutator disconnects the first coil and connects another one, which in turn is pushed by the field. In about one second, the whole thing is spinning merrily. (If everything is working!)

Since we have more parts in this type of motor, there are more possibilities for trouble. If the armature is free, if the brushes are making good contact, and so on, it works. If the armature is jammed, the motor will sit there and hum. If it's big enough, it will burn out. If the brushes are worn so badly that they don't make good contact, the motor won't run; if the brushes are jammed in their holders, same thing.

The most common problem with worn brushes, though, is heavy arcing. The motor will turn, but you'll see a great many sparks, often making a "ring of fire" all the way around the commutator. If you see this, take the brushes out and check them. Brushes must slide freely in their holders and should be smooth and shiny on the end, indicating good contact to the copper bars. If they have been arcing, the ends will be very rough, and the bars will be pitted and rough, also.

If this has happened, smooth the surface of the commutator with fine sandpaper (not emery cloth; it is conductive!) until it's bright and clean. Now get a set of new brushes, which are available at many appliance and electrical supply houses. New brushes must be exactly the same size as the originals. You can get an idea of the correct size by measuring the brush holder. As an average, the brush should be about ¼ inch shorter than the holder.

If you can't get exactly the right size, get one as close as possible, and the same shape. These can be tailored to fit by putting a piece of sandpaper flat on a table, and rubbing the brush on it, until you take off enough to make the brush fit. Try it in the holder each time you sand. The brushes should fit snugly, but they shouldn't be loose.

The actual electrical contact is made from the metal end-cap of the holder, through the "pigtail" inside the brush spring. There's a reason for this. If the current flows through the tiny springs, it can overheat them, and make them lose their tension. So we use the pigtail, and the spring does its job, holding the brush against the commutator.

Check the surface of the commutator carefully. If it's rough all the way around, the chances are that it was caused by a worn brush. However, if you can see that one or two bars are very heavily pitted and dark from arcing, with the rest of the commutator not nearly so bad, you've got trouble. One of the armature coils is either shorted or open and the armature will have to be replaced. These are so small that it is far more expensive to rewind than to buy a new one.

Most of the small brush motors used now will have the commutator connected between the field coils. There's a reason for this. The arcing of the brushes, which is always present to some extent, generates a fine loud noise in nearby radio and TV sets. The two field coils act as rf chokes, and help to keep the noise from being radiated by the ac line cord.

If this happens, clean the brushes. If this doesn't get rid of all of the noise, connect a couple of small bypass capacitors from each brush terminal to the metal frame. Something like a 0.001 uF disc ceramic capacitor, rated for at least 600V, can be added to most motors without too much trouble. Be very sure to keep the leads as short as possible, and use stout braid on the leads.

The VOM Around The Car

Here are a few handy tricks and tests you can make with a standard voltohmmeter around a car, boat, motor home or anything with a dc power supply system. The primary source of power here is a storage battery with a recharging system. These systems are about as simple as you'll get, electrically speaking. There will be a hot wire from the battery to all devices, and the frame of the vehicle itself serves as the return or ground. When the engine is running, the battery is being recharged by a generator or alternator.

Whenever you have any kind of electrical trouble, you need some way to get a handle on the problem. The first thing to check is the condition of the battery. Using the 0 to 15V or 0 to 20V dc range of the VOM, check this at any convenient point, usually at the battery itself. Normal voltage of a fully charged battery should be 12.6V. Simple test for condition of charge: Switch on a medium load, like the headlights; the voltage shouldn't drop more than a fraction of a volt. If it goes down to 8 to 10V, the battery needs recharging.

For the simplest check on whether the recharging system is working, start the engine and then read the voltage across the battery. Of course, if the battery won't turn the engine over, that answers your question. If it does start, the voltage should go up to about 14.5V. This shows that the generator or alternator is trying to charge the battery. Unfortunately, this won't tell you whether the battery will take a charge or not. The voltage regulation of the system is very good, and it won't let the voltage go higher than 14.5V or so, even on a battery with a bad cell.

You can start the engine with jumper cables from another car. There is a right and wrong way to do this, too. WATCH the POLARITY! All U.S. made cars (and a great many foreign cars) have a negative ground connection. Start the engine of the helper car first.

Connect the black cable from ground to ground on each car. Any good clean bolt, the bumper, frame, etc. makes a good contact. Now hook the red cable to the positive battery post of the good one, and to the positive battery post of the dead one. NOW try to start the engine of the car with the dead battery. This lets the generator of the helper car carry the load.

CABLE TESTING

If the car starts slowly, there may be things wrong other than a low battery. Bad contact between the battery cable terminals and the battery posts is one. To check for this, put one prod of the VOM on the end of the battery post itself, and the other on the cable terminal. Push hard to make a good contact, and then hit the starter. If you see any voltage reading at all, this contact is dirty. Use the lowest scale on the VOM for this, for accuracy. If you see 1V or more on this test, take the terminal off and clean both post and inside of the terminal. Bolt it back on very tightly. Recheck.

Second check: put one prod of the VOM on each post of the battery (not on the terminals; the post itself). Note the reading, then crank the car. The voltage should not drop below about 9 or 10 volts. If it does, the battery may be low.

If you don't get much voltage drop on the battery itself, take the same reading from the terminals. A drop here indicates a dirty contact between post and terminal; clean it up. If the voltage stays up at this point, but the starter cranks slowly, put one prod on the negative terminal of the battery and the other on a good clean bolt on the engine itself. Hit the starter. If you get any voltage reading, even on the lowest scale, the battery's ground scale isn't making good contact somewhere. You're reading a voltage drop across what should be practically a zero resistance. Loading it with the heavy current of the starter will show it up instantly.

DIM LAMPS

In some cases, lamps on the car or motor home will be mysteriously dim, though the battery checks good. This is usually due to corrosion or a dirty contact at the lamp socket. Take the bulb out, and scrape the terminals and shell. Check the socket for dirt or foreign matter.

If it's still dim, connect the negative VOM lead to the frame, and check the voltage on the hot wire at the lamp socket. If this reads the full normal voltage, take another reading, this time from the negative (shell) of the lamp socket to the nearest ground. This, of course, should be zero, if the ground connection is good.

If you see a 2 to 3V reading here, connect a jumper wire from the socket to a ground. If this brings the lamp to normal brightness, take the original ground connection off and clean it. These are generally pigtails from the socket to a nearby bolt on the frame. Many taillamps, etc. on modern cars are mounted in plastic. So, they must have a pigtail to ground to make the lamp light.

If you get a low voltage (under load) at the lamp socket, take the lamp out and repeat the test. If you now get the full battery voltage, the chances are that you have a wire somewhere with almost all of the strands broken. The low loading of the VOM will show you the full battery voltage, while the load current of the lamp causes a high voltage drop in the wire. Cure: trace the wire, looking for a place where it has been almost cut in two, or bent very sharply. In some cases, such as tail or stoplights inside the trunk, you can run another wire from the bad socket to a good one; tape the new wire to the cable, and that's all you need.

LEAKS

One of the most annoying things in the world is to go out on a cold morning and find your battery so dead that it won't even grunt. If there is a small current leakage anywhere in the system, it will drain the battery overnight. If you get it going, the next morning it could be dead again. This can be the battery itself; the only way to tell is with a "load-tester" at the service station. If the battery checks good, then you have a leakage.

If your VOM has a **dc amperes** scale, preferably up to 10.0 amps, you can use it for the next test directly. If you have only a **dc volts** scale, get a 1.0-ohm wirewound resistor, and connect the VOM prods across this, on a low **dc volts** scale. You'll read 1.0V dc for each 1.0A of current flowing through the resistor. Now you're ready to find the leakage.

Take one of the battery terminals off the post (either one). Connect the VOM between battery post and cable. Be sure that every normal load on the car is turned off, and the doors closed to turn off the dome lights. You should see zero current. If there is any leakage current, you'll read it on the meter. In my own car, some years ago, I had a steady reading of about 2.0A. This may not sound like too much, but it pulled a perfectly good battery down so far that it wouldn't even pull in the starter solenoid!

To locate the leaky device, just start disconnecting things. When you pull the wire off the guilty part, you will see the leakage current disappear. In my car, it was the stoplight switch. A new one fixed it up. The push-on terminals used in so many places in modern cars makes this a lot easier.

Multimeters

Appendix

40. General

a. A multimeter is an instrument incorporating two or more meter circuits and a meter movement in a single case. A typical multimeter contains voltmeter, ammeter, and ohmmeter circuits using a single meter movement. They may, however, be designed for many specific applications, such as measuring both resistance and capacitance, a-c voltammeters, and d-c voltmeter-millivoltmeters. The multimeters described in this chapter are those used for voltage, current, and resistance measurements.

b. To select the proper circuit for measuring voltage, current, or resistance, either a rotary selector switch or a set of pin jacks is mounted on the instrument panel. The rotary selector switch consists of many sections (wafers) of insulating material with switch contacts attached. Each position on the switch corresponds to a particular measuring circuit in the instrument. When the switch is in the d-c voltage position, for example, a contact on each wafer of the switch connects a particular element (meter movement, resistor network, or shunt) into the measuring circuit. In many multimeters, two rotary switches are used, one selecting the measuring circuit, and the other the range. The number of ranges available for the measurement of voltage, current, and resistance varies from meter to meter.

c. When two rotary switches are used, only two pin jacks are necessary on the panel of most multimeters although separate pin jacks may be provided to protect the instrument against damage on the high a-c and d-c voltage ranges. When one rotary switch is used to select the desired measuring circuit, however, separate pin jacks may be needed for each range.

d. For simplicity of reading, most multimeters have three scales, one for resistance measurements, one for d-c volts and milliamperes, and another for a-c volts. The scales usually are provided with a single set of calibration marks and with one or more sets of numerals at the major marks or dimensions. Selection of the individual ranges of measurements to be used determines the multiplying factor to be applied. For example, if the meter d-c voltage ranges are 0 to 10, 50, 250, 500, and 1,000 volts, only three calibrations are required on the indicator scale (fig. 1). The values for the 0- to 10-, 50-, and 250-volt ranges are read directly off the scale. For the 0- to 500-volt range, the 0-to-50 calibration is used, and each reading is multiplied by 10. If a value of 350 volts is being measured, the needle points to 35 on the 0-to-50 scale. Multiplying 35 by 10 gives the true value of 350 volts. Similarly, when measuring resistance with the range selector switch at the R×100 setting, each reading on the ohmmeter scale is multiplied by 100 for the true measured resistance value.

e. In general, there are two multimeters, the volt-ohm-milliammeter, and the electronic multimeter. The volt-ohm-milliammeter combines conventional voltmeter, ammeter, and ohmmeter circuits with a d'Arsonval moving-coil meter movement for d-c measurements. For a-c voltage, a rectifier is added to the circuit. The electronic multimeter combines a vacuum-tube voltmeter with conventional ammeter and ohmmeter circuits.

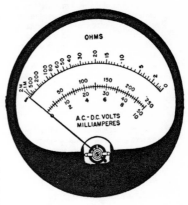

Fig. 1. Resistance, a-c, and d-c scales of typical multimeter.

41. Volt-Ohm-Milliammeter

a. GENERAL.

(1) Despite the recent advances in the design and manufacture of meters, the conventional volt-ohm-milliammeter remains the most common equipment for general electrical measurements. Most of these instruments use 50-μa to 1-ma meter movements. The 50-μa meter is used to achieve d-c voltage sensitivities of 20,000 ohms per volt, and is adequate for most d-c measurements, since circuit operation is not greatly affected. Less sensitive meters provide 1,000- or 5,000-ohms-per-volt sensitivity, but care must be taken when using these instruments that circuit operation is not upset. Most a-c voltmeter circuits are designed for 1,000 ohms per volt.

(2) The panel switches and jacks on volt-ohm-milliammeters generally have a standardized arrangement The OHMS-AC-DC switch is used to select the unit being measured. The OHMS-ZERO-ADJ knob is used to zero-adjust the meter when ohms are measured. The various jacks around the outer edge are used to select the range of resistance, voltage, or current desired. When the OHMS-AC-DC switch is in the OHMS position one test lead is inserted in the common jack and the other is inserted in the range (R$\times$1, R$\times$10, R$\times$100) desired. The leads are then shorted together and the ZERO-OHMS-ADJ knob is turned until the meter shows full-scale deflection. The unknown resistor then is placed across the two test leads and the value in ohms read directly on the meter scale. When measuring alternating or direct current or voltage, the OHMS-AC-DC switch is placed on the type of voltage or current being measured. The one test lead is inserted in the common jack and the other in the voltage or current range desired. The test leads then are applied across the voltage to be measured or in series with the circuit if current is being measured.

(3) The most common volt-ohm-milliammeters are those which measure only d-c voltage, direct current, and resistance, and those which measure a-c and d-c voltage, direct current, and resistance.

b. D-C VOLTAGE, CURRENT, AND RESISTANCE METERS.

(1) The circuit of a simple volt-ohm-milliammeter used to measure d-c voltage, current, and resistance is shown in figure 2 . The circuits and ranges are selected by using pin jacks. For current measurements less than 1 ma, the test leads are plugged into the pin jacks marked 1 MA and COMMON. The current divides between the meter and the shunt, and the meter reading is proportional to the current through it. For currents between 10 and 100 ma, the 100 MA and COMMON terminals are used. Part of the current flows through R_3 and R_4, and the rest of the current flows through R_1, R_2, and the movement. For full-scale deflection, the current through the movement is the same as before, because decreasing the shunting resistance and increasing the resistance in series with the movement causes more current to flow through the shunt and less through the meter.

(2) When measuring voltage with this instrument, the multiplier resistor used depends on the full-scale deflection required. For example, if the voltage to be measured is between 10 and 100 volts, the test leads are plugged into the 100 V and COMMON jacks. The current from the circuit under test then divides between the meter and the shunt resistors, flows through the 100,000-ohm multiplier resistor, and back to the circuit under test. The circuit operation is the same for the other two voltage positions with the exception of the multiplier resistors. Because all the resistors in this meter circuit are fixed, the current through the meter is directly proportional to the voltage across the terminals and can be read directly on the meter.

(3) For resistance measurements, either the 1 MEG jack or the one marked 100,000 OHMS is used with the COMMON jack. Depending on which jack is used, the current from either the 15-volt or the 1.5-volt battery flows through the OHMS-ZERO-ADJ resistor (R_8 or R_{10}), the resistor being measured, the meter and its shunt resistors, the multiplier resistor (R_9 or R_{11}), and back to the battery. The larger the resistor being measured, the smaller the current, and the smaller the deflection of the meter needle. The resistance scale is calibrated from right to left, and a small deflection indicates a large external resistance.

(4) The circuit of figure 2 has four direct-current ranges, three d-c voltage ranges, and two resistance ranges. Other meters of the same type may in-

clude more resistance ranges than provided here, as well as an increased number of voltage ranges. The circuit described here is limited in its application to d-c measurements. To extend its use to include a-c measurements, some type of rectifier circuit must be added.

c. A-C AND D-C VOLTAGE, DIRECT CURRENT, AND RESISTANCE METERS.

(1) Figure 3 is the circuit of a volt-ohm-milliammeter capable of measuring a-c and d-c voltages, direct current, and resistance. The voltage-measuring circuit consists of two sets of series multiplier resistors, one for d-c voltages, and the other for a-c voltages. When measuring d-c volts, the circuit selector switch is turned to the VOLTS position. One test lead then is inserted in the jack labeled COMMON and the other is plugged in the D-C VOLTS jack of the range desired. The meter movement is now shunted by the string of resistors immediately below it in the diagram, and is in series with the d-c multiplier resistors labeled D-C VOLTS.

(2) For a-c voltage measurements, the a-c multiplier resistors are used with their corresponding jacks. The germanium crystal is a half-wave rectifier feeding pulsating dc to the meter and its shunt. One test lead is inserted into the jack for the range desired and the other is inserted into the COMMON jack. When the polarity of voltage at the range jack is positive, current flows through the meter circuit. When

the current reverses and the COMMON terminal is positive, current flows through the large resistor, R_R, and the multiplier resistor. This return circuit on the negative half-cycle is necessary to keep high negative voltages off the rectifier crystal. Although the resistance of the crystal rectifier on the negative alternation is large (approximately 60,000 ohms), it still passes a small current when its polarity is reversed. Therefore, if R_R is not included in the circuit excessive voltages may damage the crystal.

(3) Current and resistance measurements are made in the manner described for the circuit of figure 3. When the R×100 jack is used, an additional battery, generally about 4.5 volts, provides enough current through the circuit for a convenient meter reading. For all resistance measurements, the test leads are plugged in the jack labeled OHMS and either the R, R×10, R×100, or R×1,000 jack, depending on the range desired.

42. Electronic Multimeter

a. GENERAL. The electronic multimeter is a vacuum-tube voltmeter circuit used to measure a-c and d-c voltages and resistance. It is similar to the vtvm in appearance, and the panel switches and jacks are the same as those used in the volt-ohm-milliammeter.

b. TYPICAL CIRCUIT.

(1) The block diagram in figure 4 is that of an electronic multimeter capable of measuring a-c and d-c voltages and

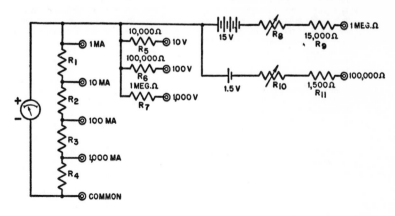

Fig. 2. D-c volt-ohm-milliammeter circuit.

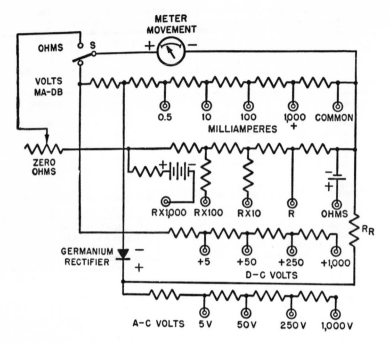

Fig. 3. Basic circuit of a-c, d-c volt-ohm-milliammeter.

resistance. For a-c voltage measurements, the a-c rectifier probe is used and pulsating dc output is fed to selector switch S_1. For d-c voltage measurements, the d-c isolating probe is used. Selector switch S_1 is a six-pole, six-position wafer switch that turns the power on and selects the type of measurement. Range switch S_2 is a four-pole, nine-position wafer switch used to obtain the desired range for each type of measurement. A d-c degenerative amplifier maintains a high input resistance and provides a low output resistance to match the resistance of the meter movement. The balancing diode, V_2, is used to buck out the contact potential of the rectifier tube in the a-c probe. The power supply furnishes d-c voltages to operate the vacuum tubes used, and the battery is part of the ohmmeter section of the multimeter.

(2) The six sections of the function selector switch are shown in the upper left portion of the complete schematic diagram in figure 5. The ON-OFF switch, S_1-7, is in the primary circuit of the power supply transformer, and the four sections of the range switch are shown in the lower left portion. The range switch is set on the 2_V-R×1 position. Section 1 of the range switch controls the balancing voltage from V_2 on a-c measurements, section 2 controls the ohmmeter circuit attenuator, and section 4 is the voltmeter section attenuator. The two-tube amplifier, V_3 and V_4, is coupled through V_5 and the low-resistance neon glow tubes, V_6 and V_7, to the indicating meter.

(3) The method of connecting the ohmmeter circuit to the amplifier is shown in figure 6. The range switch is set to position 3 (R×100). In this position, R_{34}, a 3,000-ohm resistor, is shunted across the amplifier and meter circuit. The voltage from the batteries is divided across R_{34} and the unknown resistor, and the vtvm is calibrated in terms of the voltage across R_{34}. R_3 is used to adjust the indicating meter needle to 0 before resistance measurements are made.

(4) For d-c voltage measurements, a circuit similar to the simplified one in figure 7 is used. The d-c probe contains the 5-megohm resistor used to isolate the d-c section of the multimeter and minimize the loading effect of the voltmeter on the circuit under test. The input voltage is taken off the portion of the input attenuator from R_{18} to R_{22}, and is fed to the control grid of V_3. The indicating meter reads a voltage that is proportional to the input voltage. The negative terminal of the indicating meter is connected to the common terminal of the multimeter for the $+$d-c and $\pm$d-c measurements. The positive terminal of the indicating meter is connected to COMMON for $-$d-c and a-c positions of the function selector switch. Section 4 of the function selector switch in figure 5 applies .5 ma through the indicating meter on the $\pm$d-c ranges so that the meter reads midscale for 0 volts. Section 3 of S_2 shorts out resistor R_{23} on all ranges except the 1,000-volt setting. The total input resistance for all voltage ranges except the 1,000-volt range is 20 megohms (including the probe resistor). At the 1,000-volt setting the total input resistance is 50 megohms.

(5) A-c voltage measurements are accomplished by first rectifying the ac and then applying the resultant pulsating dc to attenuator S_2-4. A portion of this voltage then is taken off the attenuator and fed to the d-c amplifier (fig. 8). The voltage used to balance out the contact potential of the probe diode, V_1, is taken from the balancing-diode voltage divider and applied to the control grid of V_4. This voltage is adjusted to equal the contact potential of V_1 applied to the grid of V_3. The instrument is calibrated to read rms volts for sinusoidal voltages. The input impedance of this instrument on all a-c ranges is 6 megohms, with a shunting capacitance of 2 micromicrofarads.

(6) When measuring current on the vtvm, only the indicating meter and the necessary shunt circuits are used. The addition of an attenuator in parallel with the meter movement makes the meter capable of measuring direct current. Generally, the attenuator is used for current measurements from .1 ma to 1,000 ma. For measurements from 1 to 10 amperes, the total attenuator resistance is in series with the meter movement, and a small resistor is shunted across the input. A separate set of pin jacks generally is used for current measurements.

c. OUTPUT POWER RANGES. The a-c output power of an audio or power amplifier can be obtained by measuring the a-c voltage across the output load resistor, squaring this value, and dividing by the value of the load resistance. Electronic multimeters capable of measuring a-c voltages usually have a scale which translates output voltage readings into relative power values in terms of decibels.

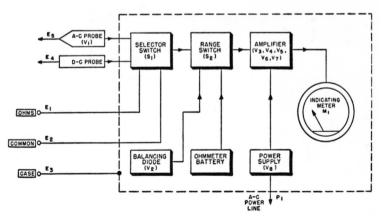

Fig. 4. Block diagram of typical electronic multimeter.

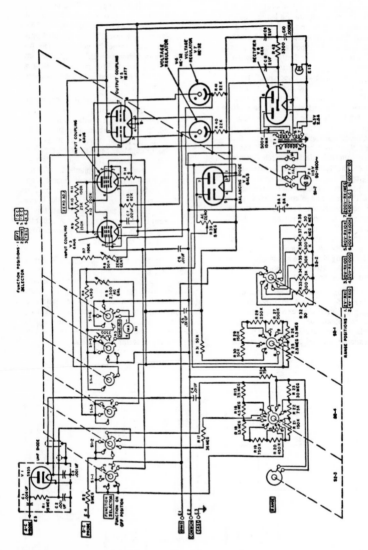

Fig. 5. Schematic diagram of typical electronic multimeter.

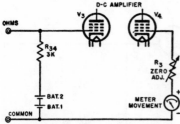

Fig. 6. Simplified schematic of ohmmeter circuit for multimeter shown in Fig. 5.

Using Multimeter

a. GENERAL PRECAUTIONS.

(1) Before using any multimeter, carefully read and observe all of the instructions covering its use in the instruction book furnished with it. When using any instrument, the front panel, particularly the area around the jacks and terminals, should be clean and dry. This prevents surface leakage which acts as a shunt and may cause an appreciable error in readings on the more sensitive ranges of the instrument.

(2) The following practices should be observed when using a multimeter on any of its ranges:

(a) When the instrument has a zero adjustment, the needle should be adjusted to 0 before any readings are taken. Electronic multimeters generally have two zero-adjust knobs on the front panel. One knob is used for setting the voltmeter to zero indication by balancing the d-c amplifier, and the other for setting the ohmmeter to indicate full-scale value with the test leads open-circuited. Multimeters of the volt-ohm-milliammeter variety do not require external zero-adjust controls for their voltage and current measuring ranges. Panel zero-adjust controls for ohmmeter circuits using batteries are always necessary to compensate for the degeneration of the batteries. If the needle cannot be brought to 0 by means of the panel adjustment knobs, additional controls usually are available within the instrument. Instructions for adjusting these controls are found in the instrument manual.

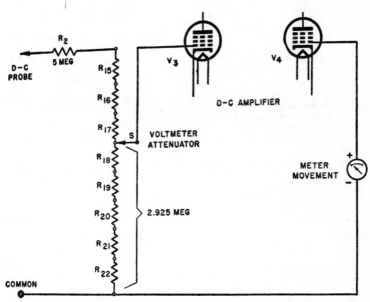

Fig. 7. Simplified d-c voltage-measuring circuit of multimeter shown in Fig. 5.

185

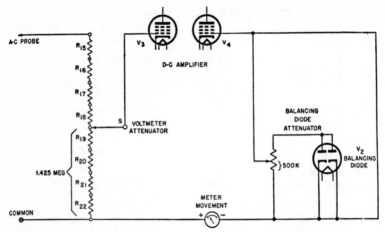

Fig. 8. Simplified schematic of a-c voltage-measuring cirucit of multimeter shown in Fig. 5.

(b) Set the range switch to the highest range for voltage or c u r r e n t measurements before making the measurement. For example, when measuring d-c voltage with a meter whose d-c voltage ranges are 0 to 10, 0 to 50, 0 to 250, 0 to 500, and 0 to 1,000, the initial range setting on the meter should be for the 0 to 1,000 range. This will protect the meter against damage from voltages which are higher than expected.

(c) When using electronic multimeters, the voltage and frequency of the power source must be within the values given in the equipment manual accompanying the instrument.

(d) Before making resistance measurements, be sure that no voltage exists in the circuit under test. *Discharge all capacitors.* The presence of any voltage through the external re-

sistance in addition to the voltage of the battery in the ohmmeter circuit can damage the meter.

(e) The rotary switches on the front panel generally are not continuously rotatable. *Do not try to force them beyond the first or last position.*

(f) Observe all of the precautions listed in the previous chapters of this manual for the prevention of damage to meters and for obtaining accuracy of readings.

b. FUNCTIONS. The multimeter is used wherever a voltmeter, ammeter, or ohmmeter is needed for trouble-shooting electronic equipment. Voltage and current measurements are made on a circuit to locate the part in which a defect exists. The ohmmeter section of the multimeter then is used for checking the value of resistors, checking capacitors for leakage, and locating grounds, short circuits, and open circuits. *The ohmmeter tests must be made with no power applied to the circuit under test.*

Summary

a. A multimeter is a single instrument consisting of a case, two or more types of measuring circuits, and an indicating meter.

b. The indicating meter used in multimeters generally has a d'Arsonval moving-coil movement.

c. The two basic multimeters are the volt-ohm-milliammeter and the electronic multimeter.

d. The volt-ohm-milliammeter uses conventional voltmeter, ammeter, and ohmmeter circuits

e. Electronic multimeters are a combination of a vacuum-tube voltmeter with conventional ammeter and ohmmeter circuits.

f. The various measuring circuits of a multimeter usually are selected by means of a rotary switch and a set of pin jacks for the test leads.

g. Two scales are necessary on the indicating meter. One scale is calibrated for the voltage and current ranges of the instrument, the other for the resistance ranges. The various ranges for each type of measurement are selected by either a rotary switch or pin jacks.

h. Volt-ohm-milliammeters generally have a sensitivity of 1,000 or 20,000 ohms per volt for voltage measurements.

i. A d-c volt-ohm-milliammeter uses a variable resistor to shunt the meter when current measurements are taken; a set of series multiplier resistors plus the shunting resistance for voltage measurements; a battery, a series resistor, and the meter-shunting resistor for resistance measurements.

j. To measure a-c voltage with the volt-ohm-milliammeter, a copper-oxide or germanium-crystal rectifier is inserted in series with the meter movement. The indicating meter gives the *average* value of the resultant pulsating dc and is calibrated in terms of *rms* volts.

k. A typical electronic multimeter consists of an a-c rectifier probe, a d-c isolating probe, a shunt and series resistance network, a d-c amplifier, a d'Arsonval-type meter movement, and a power-supply circuit. A conventional ohmmeter circuit is included to measure resistance.

l. When using a multimeter, observe all the precautions listed in the equipment manual, as well as all the other precautions necessary for protection of the meter.

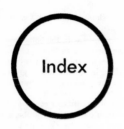

Index

E

F

G

M

N

O

P